CHOCOLATE BARS AND RUBBER BOOTS

THE SMALLWOOD INDUSTRIALIZATION PLAN

by
Doug Letto

Blue Hill Publishing
Paradise, Newfoundland
1998

CHOCOLATE BARS AND RUBBER BOOTS

THE SMALLWOOD INDUSTRIALIZATION PLAN

by
Doug Letto

Blue Hill Publishing
Paradise, Newfoundland
1998

Cover Design: Beth Oberholtzer

Printed by:
Robinson-Blackmore Printing and Publishing
St. John's, Newfoundland, Canada

∝ Printed on acid-free paper

Published by: Blue Hill Publishing
P.O. Box 18 — Site 14 — RR #2
Paradise, Newfoundland, Canada
A1L 1C2

Canadian Cataloguing in Publication Data

Letto, Douglas Mervyn, 1958-

Chocolate bars and rubber boots

Includes bibliographical references
ISBN 0-9684326-0-3

1. Industrial policy — Newfoundland — History — 20th century.
2. Industrialization — Newfoundland — History — 20th century.
3. Manufacturing industries — Newfoundland — History — 20th century.
I. Title

HC117.N4L45 1998   338.09718'09'045   C98-950259-7

TABLE OF CONTENTS

ACKNOWLEDGEMENTS

This work would not have been possible without the help of Dr. David Close and Dr. Peter Boswell from the Department of Political Science at Memorial University.

Bert Riggs and Gail Weir of Memorial's Newfoundland Studies Archives were helpful and accommodating in my search for documents from the Smallwood Collection. Bert volunteered, and I gratefully accepted, his offer to proofread this work when it constituted my masters thesis in political science.

My wife, Joan, offered encouragement and motivated me to keep going until this work was finished. Of course, she's an old hand at this business, having completed her own masters thesis in biochemistry with two small children underfoot. Aimee and Douglas patiently waited for me to finish "just one more page" before I went on to more important things, like Lego's and games of Clue, and even live theatre in which they had starring roles. This book is dedicated to the three of them.

The mistakes of course, are mine.

Introduction

The February 9, 1950 memo from Richardson Woods, a Chicago consultant, to economist Stacey May of Nelson Rockerfeller's IBEC, provided a snapshot of an impatient Joseph Smallwood, Newfoundland's first premier. Woods' memo noted Smallwood's "great sense of urgency about economic development" and it reported "he grudges every week that passes without constructive action".[1]

In the months following, Smallwood had the IBEC Technical Services Group undertake a "survey" of the province's economic prospects. A press release from the IBEC Group described the survey as "a broad investigation of the economic resources of the Province, with special attention to world market analysis."[2] Smallwood though, was already looking beyond the IBEC report, telling Newfoundlanders with typical overstatement,

> A mere hundred million dollars invested in the development of our resources would absorb every last bit of our man-power (sic) and create a man-power shortage.[3]

But it was manufacturing, not natural resource development, to which Smallwood would first commit himself. In the 22 months between June 1950 and March 1952, Smallwood's "great sense of urgency" would translate itself into the establishment of, or commitment to, 16 new manufacturing industries, including a cement plant, and chocolate, leather, glove and textile factories.

The Newfoundland Government launched these industries through its Economic Development Department and the Department's Director General, Dr. Alfred Valdmanis. Valdmanis, a former Latvian finance minister, was recruited by Smallwood

---

1   Memo, Richardson Woods to Stacey May of International Basic Economy Commission's Technical Services Group, February 9, 1950. J.R. Smallwood Collection, Centre for Newfoundland Studies, Memorial University. File 3.08.336 [In subsequent citations, this collection of material will be referred to as JRS Collection.]
2   Ibid
3   J.R. Smallwood Speech, 1950 (undated). File 7.02.003. JRS Collection

while Valdmanis worked in Ottawa for the federal government. As Newfoundland's economic czar, Valdmanis' role was to travel — mostly to Europe — to make contact and reach tentative agreements with companies or individuals interested in establishing enterprises in Newfoundland. The agreements were subject to cabinet approval, a near automatic assumption in those days.

Smallwood's public comments exuded near missionary zeal as he promoted economic development in Newfoundland. In the 1950 legislature debate on establishing the Department of Economic Development, Smallwood uttered his famous "develop or perish" statement, and he related a story he told a Toronto newspaper reporter in 1948, while negotiating the Terms of Union in Ottawa.

> I used to tell him I'd be Premier of Newfoundland and that there'd be no difficulty of that. And he used to laugh, and I used to say, 'don't laugh'. I said 'whoever is Premier of Newfoundland has to do one thing, he has to develop Newfoundland or be booted out'.[4]

Smallwood promised his approach to industrialization would be calculated and orderly. Harold Horwood, a Liberal backbencher in the first Assembly after Confederation, and a close ally of Smallwood in the Confederation campaign, wrote years later the plan was to develop the industries one at a time, sell them to the private sector, and use the proceeds to start more industries.[5]

In reality though, the pragmatic, snail's-pace approach promised by the government, appeared to be only for public consumption. In fact, the government was moving more quickly. This was borne out in a memo from Alfred Valdmanis to Smallwood on May 11, 1951, on the eve of Valdmanis' departure for Europe, a trip where he planned to negotiate six new industries.[6]

---

4 Peter Neary. The Political Economy of Newfoundland, 1929-1972. (Toronto: Copp Clark) 1973. pp. 194-195
5 Harold Horwood. Joey. Toronto: Stoddart 1989. p. 171
6 Memo, Alfred Valdmanis to J.R. Smallwood, Department of Economic Development. File 3.08.002. JRS Collection

The industries themselves were to be capitalized with 50% government financing through an attractive loan guarantee program. The terms did not require a cash investment on the part of the investors as a prerequisite to qualify for the guarantees. Investors were given the option to make their investment "in cash or kind". This meant they could gain access to the loan guarantee program without investing a penny of their own money. Not surprisingly, given that German industrialists had suffered heavy losses through six years of war, all chose the "in kind" route, an option that was intended to include everything from "know-how, machinery, or any material, engineering supervision, erection, building, etc." and would be matched dollar for dollar by the Newfoundland Government in the form of guaranteed bank loans.[7]

Without exception, the industries lost money. This cost the Newfoundland treasury dearly. Not only was their startup financed through the public treasury, most had to be sustained with additional government loans and grants. This eventually put pressure on Smallwood's government to hire a consultant to assess the industries.

In 1957, seven years after the program began, the government-commissioned consultant's report recommended some of the industries be closed and it proposed changes in the way others were managed. The Corner Brook-based gypsum and cement plants, built on locally available resources and geared toward the local construction market, remained going concerns. Those industries however, have long since passed from government to private control. Indeed, a few short years after the program began, the government de-emphasized the rush toward establishing manufacturing industries, and began to concentrate instead on fisheries development.[8] Without exception though, Newfoundland taxpayers financed all sixteen industries under Smallwood's plan.

This book is not a study on regional development, rather it is an examination of a specific initiative undertaken by the Newfoundland government during its early years as a province

---

7   Ibid, File 3.08.002
8   Memo, Gordon Pushie to J.R. Smallwood, 1957. File 3.08.033. JRS Collection

of Canada. This policy, which entailed significant public investment, happened in the climate of post-war economic thinking, which both in Britain and Canada, implied a vital role for government in the area of economic planning. During this period, Britain developed a large nationalized industrial sector and it implemented major social welfare reform with the National Health Service.[9] In Canada, the 1945 White Paper on Employment and Income advocated the maintenance of "high and stable levels of employment and income" as "a primary aim of government policy in the postwar period."[10] This focus on generating high levels of employment was seen as being influenced by developments in Britain, and by the poverty experienced in Canada during the depression. These developments led in Canada to the strengthening of the Department of Finance as an instrument of financial control and of the Department of Health and Welfare in the area of social policy.[11]

The developments in Ottawa also served to legitimize a larger role for the state in the planning of the economy. While there is little direct evidence Smallwood was influenced by these events, he had to look no farther than Newfoundland's high unemployment and large emigration numbers to appreciate the need for some type of intervention by his government. Harold Horwood, his ally in the Confederation campaign, argues Smallwood's socialist and populist bent, and his conclusion about the "evil of capitalism", were formed during the early 1920's, when Smallwood wrote for Socialist newspapers in New York[12]. Indeed, Smallwood saw the situation in Newfoundland in 1949 as a continuation of the old story of underdevelopment. And he appeared to be philosophically inclined to engage the treasury in the pursuit of industry to ameliorate such conditions. He underlined his resolve in a speech to the legislature in the fall of 1949.

9 Shonfield, Andrew. Modern Capitalism [The Changing Balance of Public and Private Power] New York: Oxford University Press. 1976. pp.88-89
10 Phidd, Richard W. and G. Bruce Doern. The Politics and Management of Canadian Economic Policy. Toronto: Macmillan. 1978. p.159
11 Ibid
12 Horwood, pp. 30-38

...we might take some of the surplus...and put it behind some movement for the development of this province...That is the only permanent solution to the age-old problem that began officially in 1832 and has never ceased except during the First Great War and during the Second Great War.[13]

This work will focus on the industrialization program, with a view to detailing the activities of the industries, and providing an analysis of the way in which the program and specific industries were managed. As a preliminary point, the program, despite an enormous expenditure that amounted to two-thirds of the pre-Confederation surplus[14], has been the subject of limited study. One possible reason is that key documents from that era have only recently become available. This is especially so with respect to the Smallwood Collection in Memorial University's Centre for Newfoundland Studies.

The industrialization program, though enthusiastically supported by Smallwood and others, was poorly planned and too hastily embarked upon. There appeared to be no set of goals and objectives to guide development, apart from Smallwood's credo of "develop or perish". While the first three industries — the cement, gypsum, and hardwoods plants — were based on local resources and directed toward the local market, Smallwood did not offer a firm explanation why Newfoundland should become involved in the other industries, which were based on the import of raw materials and geared toward exporting into already North American competitive markets.

The main weakness in the program however, was the loan guarantee program that provided and delivered substantial

---

13 Proceedings, October 17, 1949. p.413
14 Proceedings, November 30, 1949. pp.846-848. The pre-Confederation surplus refers to the balance for the Newfoundland government at the time it joined Canada. There are various references in print to a surplus ranging from $40 million to $49 million. This book uses the figure $40,283,147. This number is taken from the first budget speech of the Smallwood government on November 30, 1949. In recounting for the House the details of the new province's financial standing, the Minister of Finance, H.W. Quinton noted that the surplus at Confederation was $47,676,482., minus liabilities of $7,393,335. These liabilities included accounts payable, trustee stock, savings certificates, and both public debt and savings certificate interest.

financial help to industries, based not on rigorous study and analysis by experts, but on the blessing and recommendation of the new Province's economic czar, Alfred Valdmanis. The loan guarantee program enabled business people who were unaccustomed to the North American market, access to millions of dollars in scarce government money, while requiring little more than their own ideas and expertise in return. This cannot merely be seen as a technical weakness, but rather, as a political mistake which in six short years, consumed $26 million,[15] and millions of dollars more in unpaid interest charges.

This book will place the Newfoundland industrialization plan in the context of what was happening in Nova Scotia at about the same time. The decision to include the Nova Scotia case centres around some of the similarities it has with Newfoundland. Like Newfoundland, Nova Scotia has lagged behind the nation in important indicators of economic growth; it was primarily a resource-based economy; it was outside the industrial centre of Canada and North America, though not as far removed from the centre as Newfoundland; and Nova Scotia and Newfoundland, as provinces of Canada, have identical constitutional powers. These similarities should not be taken to mean that any given business would have an equal chance of surviving in both provinces. Indeed, an argument could be made that Nova Scotia would have a major locational advantage over Newfoundland when it comes to getting manufactured goods to market. The Nova Scotia case also serves to illustrate that Newfoundland was not alone when it came to directing industrial development.

The Newfoundland and Nova Scotia cases are consistent with the global experience, where countries and regions on the periphery of larger trading partners have adopted similar measures to jump-start economic development, often with catastrophic consequences for their treasuries.

This book was possible because of an assortment of primary and secondary materials. The chief primary materials are contained in the Smallwood Collection in the Centre for Newfound-

---

15 This represents in excess of $150 million in 1998 dollars.

land Studies at Memorial University. These include Department of Economic Development documents, including memoranda to cabinet in support of the establishment of the various industries. The departmental documents also contain correspondence between Alfred Valdmanis and the banking houses, correspondence between Valdmanis and J.R. Smallwood, and internal memoranda on the operation and status of the various industries established under the government plan.

The Smallwood Collection also contains annual reports of the Industrial Development Loan Board, and reports and memoranda involving the International Basic Economy Commission.

Proceedings of the House of Assembly comprise an important record of the 'cut and thrust' of debate on industrialization and other public policy issues.

There was substantial coverage of the Newfoundland development program in the newspapers and journals of the day. The *Evening Telegram* gave considerable coverage of the promise the new industries held for Newfoundland. The paper's editorial writers and columnist Harold Horwood (who had by now left politics) questioned Smallwood's approach to economic development. The Board of Trade Journal provided a business perspective on the increased competition at the time of Confederation, with much of its space devoted to the problems Newfoundland-based manufacturers encountered while making the transition to the Canadian market. The Toronto-based Financial Post also gave extensive coverage to the Newfoundland economic situation. In the early stages, the Post detailed the opportunities Confederation presented for Canadian business, and later, as the industrialization program got underway, the paper gave considerable space to analysing the prospects of the new industries.

1

Confederation: The Beginnings of an Industrialization Policy

At the stroke of midnight, March 31, 1949, Britain's oldest colony became Canada's tenth and youngest province. The union brought Canada's array of social programs — old age pensions, war veteran's pensions, family allowances and unemployment insurance — to the 350,000 people of Newfoundland and Labrador. Union with Canada meant something else as well. It broke down the customs and immigration barrier between Newfoundland and Canada. Soon after, Canadian manufacturers would successfully compete with Newfoundland manufacturers who had previously enjoyed tariff protection courtesy of the government in St. John's.

For Newfoundlanders generally, union with Canada eased the movement west. Even before the immigration barriers came down in the two years before Confederation though, 4900 Newfoundlanders migrated to Canada.[1] The migration factor was a central feature in several speeches given in the early 1950's by the new Premier, Joseph Smallwood. The migration phenomenon also appeared to give impetus to his search for new industry. Returning from a six-week trip to Europe to attract business to Newfoundland, Smallwood told a Newfoundland radio audience,

> We must develop or perish. We must develop or our people will go in the thousands to other parts of Canada. We must create new jobs, or our young men especially will go off to other places to get the jobs they can't get here.

1 Neary, p. 185

Develop, develop, develop ——that's been my slogan and that will remain my slogan.[2]

In a 1951 speech to the House, Smallwood again detailed his fear about emigration, and how "confederation with Canada contained the dire threat of accelerating vastly and spectacularly that outward flow of people.[3] In the same speech, he outlined the need for the industrialization program his government had already initiated.

> Something had to be done, and done quickly. Our people had to be persuaded that Newfoundland itself, as a result of Confederation, was embarked upon a new course ...Newfoundland would go ahead. Opportunities would spring up in this province.[4]

Smallwood may have been echoing what business leaders and the newspapers reported. The Newfoundland Board of Trade was said to be so concerned about "almost wholesale migration from Newfoundland", that it asked the government in May 1950 to investigate the matter.[5] The Evening Telegram wrote in the autumn of 1950, that "many hundreds of Newfoundlanders have moved out of the Province, if reports from railwaymen and others are to be believed".[6]

But not everyone saw emigration as a problem. H.B. Mayo, a former Newfoundlander then teaching political science at the University of Alberta, suggested in 1951 that 100,000 people leave Newfoundland - that "it is better to have in Newfoundland 250,000 healthy and prosperous people than twice that number at near-subsistence level."[7] Mayo recommended converting most of the island to a National Park, and he was critical of people mistaking post-Confederation advances for real progress.

---

2 Speech by Joseph R. Smallwood, October 12, 1952. File 7.02.003. JRS Collection
3 File 7.02.004. JRS Collection. [Undated]
4 Ibid
5 Bassler, Gerhard P. "Develop or Perish: Joseph R. Smallwood and Newfoundland's Quest for German Industry, 1949-1953". Acadiensis. Volume XV, No.2. Spring 1986, 92-113. p.99
6 Ibid, p. 98
7 H.B. Mayo. "The Future of Newfoundland -Is the Island Overpopulated?", in Atlantic Guardian, Vol. VIII, No.3, 14-19. March 1951, p. 19

On the one hand, some people see the province growing in population and prosperity, with all the improvements in health, education and other public services, that prosperity can bring. It is a pleasant and rosy picture - but painted from a one-sided view. From another viewpoint may be seen a future in which the population is growing faster than jobs can be found; with thousands of fishermen under-employed and earning less than a decent livelihood.[8]

Mayo's essay was provocative. A month after his commentary appeared in the *Atlantic Guardian*, the paper printed a rebuttal from Alfred Valdmanis. Valdmanis went on the offensive, suggesting a five-year national plan of concessions and freight rate reductions to allow Newfoundland to "catch up". He argued under such circumstances, Newfoundland could properly develop its farming industry on the west coast; build a new paper mill based on timber from Labrador; hydro projects could be started; and new mines opened.[9] So confident was Valdmanis of his plan, that he predicted "as from the spring of 1952 on, there won't be further unemployment in Newfoundland."[10]

Many thousands of Newfoundlanders had discovered for themselves the lack of opportunity at home. While "the drain was temporarily stopped" between 1951 and 1956, an average of 3,300 Newfoundlanders left the province yearly between 1956 and 1961.[11] The Royal Commission on the Economic State and Prospects lamented in 1967,

...those leaving the Province in the past appear to have been mostly the highest skilled and most dynamic, very people, in fact, who have the training and enterprise to generate additional employment for others. Furthermore, those leaving the Province have tended to be the younger

---

8 Ibid, p. 14
9 Alfred Valdmanis in Atlantic Guardian, April 1951. Vol.VIII, No.4, 11-17. p.16
10 Ibid, pp.16-17
11 Report of the Royal Commission on the Economic State and Prospects of Newfoundland and Labrador, St. John's. 1967. p.11 (As a percentage of the population that migrated, the 1956-61 period is second only to the five year period 1992-97, in the post-Confederation era. This latter period is the time immediately following the moratorium on cod and other groundfish.)

members of the work force, which adds to the proportion-
ate number of young and old who have to be cared for by
the remaining labour force.[12]

Unemployment was not a new phenomenon to Newfoundland. The situation in 1949 however, was exacerbated by a
combination of internal and external factors. There were layoffs
in the logging industry brought about by a downturn in the
pulp and paper sector, and layoffs on the American bases as the
United States cut back its defense spending in Newfoundland.
The fishery was a near failure in 1949; the devaluation of the
British pound in the summer of that year hurt exports of Bell
Island iron ore to the United Kingdom.[13] As if that was not
enough to upset the Newfoundland economy, local manufacturing firms faced stiff competition from Canadian manufactured goods that now entered Newfoundland tariff-free.

The Newfoundland Journal of Commerce - the newspaper
of the Newfoundland Board of Trade - described the stiff competition firms faced from mainland companies in the post-Confederation era. In September 1949, the Board reported "one
manufacturer told The Journal that the joining of Newfoundland with the mainland has greatly increased competition for
the clothing manufacturers here from Montreal and Toronto
firms." The report continued,

Since union Newfoundland has been overrun at times by
clothing agents who visited all or most of the large settle-
ments seeking business and offering goods at a little less
than the local prevailing price.[14]

Mainland firms brought competition to other sectors as
well. A month later, The Journal reported on the Drug and Toilet
Sector trade.

They have been solicited by travelling agents from various
comparatively unknown mainland firms. Like other businessmen, shortly before union and since, they have been
the target of intensified selling campaigns organized by

12 Ibid, p. 22
13 Bassler, p. 49
14 Newfoundland Journal of Commerce, Vol. XVI, No. 9. September 1949. p. 19

mainland firms which have no conception of the limited scope of the Newfoundland market.[15]

Increased competition took a toll on Newfoundland manufacturers. While some bravely vowed to "not desist in their efforts to improve their plants and thereby keep abreast of even the keenest competition from the mainland", there was acknowledgement that at least in the footwear trade, some companies were having a tough time.

One local manufacturer closed his operations a few weeks before union was consummated. The other, the Newfoundland Boot and Shoe Company, Ltd., in Harbour Grace, is continuing production.[16]

Huge mainland firms put on a push in the manufacture of foodstuffs such as biscuits, candy and margarine. "Confederation gave the local biscuit industry a severe wound", the Journal reported in August 1955, "one plant, manufacturing English biscuits, closed down."[17] The local candy trade was described as being virtually "extinct"[18] and mainland margarine firms "are advertising their product quite extensively here."[19]

The availability of Canadian goods gave Newfoundland consumers something they had not previously experienced — choice. According to the Journal, the availability of new products was exerting a change on consumers, who were now "shopping around".[20] Increased competition from the mainland firms affected manufacturers too. The Journal reported in August 1955, "the biscuit manufacturers realize how important it is to 'dress up' their product. 'Dressing up' was at a minimum before Confederation."[21]

Those mainland firms the Newfoundland Board of Trade reported on, were filling the Journal's pages with advertisements. Some mainland companies had engaged Newfoundland

15 Journal, Vol. XVI, No. 10. October 1949. p. 17
16 Ibid, p. 19
17 Ibid, p. 7
18 Journal, Vol. XVI, No.5. May 1950. p.21
19 Ibid, p. 8
20 Journal, Vol.XV, No.9. September 1949, p. 19
21 Journal, Vol. XXVI, No. 8. August 1955 p. 7

agents to sell and distribute their products, but many more appeared to operate out of head office. From Montreal companies selling windows, to a Hamilton firm marketing water pumps, to the Great West Felt Co. in Elmira, Ontario with its eye-catching message — "it is our responsibility and business to warm your feet with Great West All Wool Felt Footwear", Newfoundland was virgin territory for people wanting to make a dollar.

It was evident that Canadian businesses viewed Newfoundland as a substantial market in which to do additional business. The Financial Post published several articles detailing the size of the Newfoundland market and its potential for new business. "We Can Double Sales to Island" trumpeted the Post in the days before March 31, 1949, noting the end of tariffs in Newfoundland would mean an additional $30-$45 million worth of business to Canadian firms, chiefly as a result of displacing "one half to one third of the purchases which Newfoundland now makes in United States..."[22] The Post's readers were told that many of Newfoundland's 75 manufacturing firms and their 3,500 workers "may now find themselves at a disadvantage against Canadian competition" given that the Newfoundland firms were small and were required to use imported "high-cost raw materials".[23] Newfoundland would be an important market for "foods, clothing, radios, machinery, automobiles, washing machines" once Confederation removed duties that were as high as 60%."[24]

But what of the impact on Newfoundland firms? How would they adjust in the aftermath of the dismantling of the tariff walls?

Newfoundland firms were promised special assistance to help in the transition to provincehood. After much wrangling, the federal government agreed to a preferential premium of 15-percent on contracts tendered by Newfoundland firms. This would be reduced to 10-percent by March 31, 1951 and eliminated by March 31, 1952.[25] Some local firms did get federal

22 *Financial Post*. March 23, 1949. p. 13
23 Ibid, p. 16
24 Ibid, p. 16
25 Raymond B. Blake. <u>Canadians at Last: Canada Integrates Newfoundland as a</u>

government business, but the Post concluded "it will take more than that to aid the firms which are badly hurt by mainland competition."[26]

The Conservative Opposition in the legislature attempted to exploit the concern some Newfoundlanders showed about competition from mainland Canadian firms. Speaking on the unemployment issue in October 1949, Conservative leader John G. Higgins referred to the competition Newfoundland firms faced from Canadian mail order companies.

> There are clerks and shop-keepers. Will the mail order business put these men out of work? We know well enough that the mail order business contributes very little to this country;...[27]

In the same speech, Higgins attacked the practice of importing produce from Prince Edward Island.

> Now at the present moment, the markets are flooded with Prince Edward Island produce, and this produce undersells our local farmers...for years, Prince Edward Island has been sending stuff into this country and has not bought a single thing from us. As far as we are concerned, Prince Edward Island is useless to us,...[28]

This kind of statement exposed the ambivalence some in Newfoundland maintained toward Confederation. Smallwood, however, was not one of those doubters. He regularly hauled out the train of benefits to describe how Confederation had made Newfoundland better off. Speaking in the legislature on a bill to establish the Department of Economic Development, he talked about "the great system of social security developed in Canada", including "family allowances, old age security, pensions for the blind, unemployment insurance, improved and increased benefits for war veterans, national housing..."[29]

Smallwood viewed the array of Canadian social programs as a supplement to jobs, rather than a substitute for employ-

Province. (Toronto: University of Toronto Press) 1994. pp.106-108
26 Financial Post, July 1949
27 House of Assembly Proceedings, October 27, 1949. p. 533
28 Ibid, p. 533
29 Proceedings, July 18, 1949. p. 49

ment. This position was evident in the same debate on establishing the Department of Economic Development, where Smallwood noted social programs "at most...could blunt the sharp edge of extreme poverty in certain classes of our population" and what was needed was development of Newfoundland's natural resources "to yield the basic conditions of a higher standard of living for our people."[30]

Despite that long-term goal, Smallwood was well aware of the immediate role social programs played in augmenting people's income. A report his government commissioned in preparation for its arguments on changing the financial terms of union with Canada, showed Newfoundlanders consistently earning less per capita than other Atlantic Canadians and only slightly more than half of the Canadian average.[31] The same report showed nearly twice as many Newfoundland families in the lowest income categories compared to the Canadian average.[32] Newfoundlanders lagged far behind other Canadians too in terms of educational attainment, and creature comforts, such as furnace-heated homes, hot and cold water, flush toilets, baths or showers and telephones.[33]

That standard of living, and more particularly, the employment situation, came sharply into focus in the first autumn after Confederation. Speaking in the Legislature, Smallwood said "...unemployment, and indeed destitution, have begun to show themselves again in Newfoundland." Citing a near failure in the fishery and problems in the pulp and paper industry that would increase unemployment among loggers, Smallwood predicted it would cost

---

30 Ibid, pp. 49-50
31 H. Karl Goldenberg. Interim Report on Capacity to Pay and Comparative Tax Burden in Newfoundland and the Maritime Provinces. Presented to the Newfoundland Commission Revision of Financial Terms. St. John's. January 1956. pp. 10-13. [Goldenberg, an economist and labour lawyer, was economic advisor to the Government of Newfoundland during the work of this Commission and during Smallwood's own Commission set up three years earlier in 1953. In his book I Chose Canada, Smallwood stated the Newfoundland Commission was really an effort to prepare the province's case for continuing the transitional grant, intended at Confederation to allow Newfoundland to provide public services at reasonable levels of taxation. This is now referred to as the Term 29 award.]
32 Ibid, p. 14
33 Ibid, p. 22

...somewhere between a million and a million and a half dollars to pay welfare to able-bodied Newfoundlanders from October to March.[34]

By the time the numbers were tallied in the next spring, able-bodied relief had cost $3.4-million, more than double Smallwood's estimate.

The juxtaposition of Newfoundland's jobless against the prospects for better times, increasingly became the centrepiece of Smallwood's speeches. Addressing the legislature on the necessity of spending some of the $40-million Commission of Government surplus to survey Newfoundland's resource potential, Smallwood implored the Opposition to understand what was at stake for Newfoundlanders.

A year or two from now, the Opposition may be holding this Government up to ridicule, and we will have to hang our heads for having flung away and wasted $200,000 of the Public's money, but we are going to take a chance if the House is willing....People are not going to wait forever for this development; if we don't give it to them tomorrow, they get more and more out of jobs and pull up their stakes; you can't blame them, and they beg or borrow money to get out of Newfoundland and go where jobs are, you can't blame them. Our job is to back them; go right out, boots and all, make or break. Here, what I mean by "make or break", here is gamble.[35]

The Opposition accused Smallwood of acting in haste as he put through legislation to create the Department of Economic Development. Conservative leader Higgins decried the lack of information about the state of the new province's finances.

I do not think we can find out where we are and whither we are tending unless we know exactly the financial position of this country....I quite agree with Major Cashin that no further discussions should be carried on in connection with Bills already brought before the House, and that no

---

34 Proceedings, October 19, 1949. p. 411
35 Proceedings, March 30, 1950. p. 489

further Bills should be brought here unless we know exactly what the financial position is.[36]

In some respects, Smallwood appeared to be pursuing development with caution. This was in sharp contrast to how he would proceed later. In announcing legislation in the fall of 1949 to establish a provincial lending agency called the Industrial Development Loan Board to deal with applications for "twenty or thirty or fifty thousand dollars, or maybe more", the government attempted to comfort the opposition and the public that the money would not be wasted. Smallwood stipulated " these loans would of course be properly secured." It was clear as well though, that the government envisaged some risk, as the loans would "deal with a type of enterprise which the ordinary chartered bank does not..."[37]

At the same time, the government grappled with how best to use the surplus handed to it by the Commission of Government at Confederation. Smallwood told the legislature the government was leaning toward subdividing two-thirds of the amount (he estimated about $25-million) for "developmental purposes", among various areas of government, including school and hospital construction, "so much for fishery development; so much, perhaps for agricultural development..." (Term 24 of the Terms of Union between Newfoundland and Canada required two-thirds of the surplus be used for "the development of resources and for the establishment or extension of public services"; the other one third was required to be placed on deposit at the Bank of Canada to be spent on current account so as to "facilitate the maintenance and improvement of Newfoundland public services.)"[38] Smallwood saw it necessary to allot the funds "so that the surplus would not be frittered away..."[39] In time however, much of the surplus would be exhausted, not on school and hospital construction, or fisheries and agricultural development, but on a highly questionable industrial development plan.

---

36 Proceedings, July 18, 1954. p. 54
37 Proceedings, October 23, 1949. p. 451
38 Proceedings, March 31, 1952. p. 24
39 Proceedings, October 23, 1949. p. 450

FUNDING INDUSTRIAL DEVELOPMENT

The government's first vehicle to fund local industrial development, the Industrial Development Loan Board (IDLB) never
achieved its objectives to provide funding for - as Smallwood
put it - "both the big and the little man". Nearly a year after it
was established, the Board reported it had not disbursed any
loans. It seemed most applicants wanted loans to pay off debts
or purchase personal items such as motor cars. Adding to the
problems, many did not have legal title to the property they
offered as collateral. The Board discovered that many of the
people who made applications did not have equity capital, and
as a result, they were denied assistance.[40]

Subsequent reports from the Board revealed few people
applying for assistance at all -just six applications in 1952-53,
compared to 52 in the first two years of the program.[41] The
Board reported on "the succession of approaches for assistance
pertaining to purposes outside the Board's operations...."[42] Five
years into the program, just 20 loans totalling $147,550 dollars
had been disbursed. The Board noted that during 1955, lending
activity "was again restricted" because of "the relatively limited
number of sound approaches which qualified.."[43]

Far from meeting Smallwood's early objectives of providing
funding "for the big and little man", the IDLB served to under-
line a lack of commitment on the part of the government to
encourage Newfoundlanders to start businesses or expand existing ones. This can be the only conclusion given the repetition
of the factors which barred local applicants from securing assistance, and the comparative ease with which Europeans obtained   government   loans   under   the   government's
industrialization program.

Smallwood was determined to act against this early post-
Confederation backdrop of the slow pace of development.

In the spring of 1950, he made one of the most significant
moves of his young government. Smallwood hired Alfred Vald-

---

40 Second Annual Report, Industrial Development Loan Board, March 31, 1952. p.
   4
41 Third Annual Report, Industrial Development Loan Board. March 31, 1953
42 Ibid
43 Third Annual Report, March 31, 1950. p. 5.

manis to be his Director of Economic Development. A former
Latvian Finance Minister, Valdmanis charmed Smallwood with
both his manner and his vision for an industrialized Newfoundland. Prior to his arrival in Newfoundland, Valdmanis had
worked for the Nova Scotia Research Foundation, where he had
assessed the feasibility of establishing gypsum and cement
industries in that province.[44] While those projects did not go
ahead in Nova Scotia, they became the first initiatives Valdmanis pursued in Newfoundland. The government approved
the cement project first and then the gypsum proposal, both at
Corner Brook.

Valdmanis impressed Smallwood with his drive and his
contacts, leading Smallwood to say he loved Valdmanis as he
could never love a brother or sister.

Valdmanis was intent on charting his own path. He was not
impressed with the work Nelson Rockerfeller's IBEC had done
for Smallwood. This was underlined in a memo to Smallwood
in December 1950, just six months after being named Director
General. Valdmanis claimed, in typical dramatic terms, IBEC's
calculations for a proposed $66-million, 500 tons per day paper
mill for Bay D'Espoir would result in "a dismal, if not a criminal,
failure."[45]

Valdmanis appeared ready to set the groundwork to establish with Smallwood his own credentials as the economic czar of
Newfoundland. He elaborated in a letter to Smallwood, on the
proposed third paper mill, which would consume wood logged
in Labrador.

I may be able to bring into Newfoundland such a mill at,
say, 45 million dollars, and such a mill should prove a
tremendous success.[46]

Valdmanis did not appear to suffer from lack of confidence.
This was evident in a letter he wrote Smallwood, where he
praised the Premier for choosing the Latvian as Director of
Economic Development.

---

44 Bassler, p. 107
45 Note, contained in letter from Alfred Valdmanis to J.R. Smallwood, December
    12, 1950. Note #1. File 6.00.005. JRS Collection
46 Ibid

It is something more which leads me to these almost incredible contracts we have already signed or may have in preparation, and this "something" is even hard to define. That is the knowledge, the skilled brain, the skill to master the subject plus a commanding impression plus wide connections with the best firms in the world.

I think I have all this.[47]

During 1951, Smallwood assured the legislature he would take a prudent approach to dealing with the province's surplus. The government though, was actually still undecided about how to fund the industrialization drive to which it had become committed. Notwithstanding this indecision, the government had fully financed the cement, gypsum and hardwood industries to the tune of several million dollars.

It is evident from the Valdmanis papers, that some cabinet ministers were cool to the idea of direct government financing for industrial development, and concerned about the prospects of finding private sector owners for the plants. In some cases, Valdmanis felt there was outright hostility. In a letter from New York, he related to Smallwood a conversation with cabinet minister H.W. Quinton in a corridor at Colonial Building following Valdmanis' submission of a report promoting the development of a 100,000 ton cement mill. He quoted Quinton as saying "I am going to object to any kind of government enterprise. Surely you can build the plant, but how are you going to get rid of it?"[48] Valdmanis noted that Smallwood had done everything he could to help with economic development, but the cabinet did not seem to be as helpful.

"From you, yourself, my Premier, I have the highest regard...there may be a few more Cabinet Ministers who may be mentioned in the same breath. But the Cabinet as such?? I do not dare to guess, I think indirectly, but clearly, an answer has been given to me."[49]

These were the early days of the Smallwood/Valdmanis

47 Ibid
48 Ibid, Note #1, p. 1
49 Ibid, Letter

partnership, and while Valdmanis was unsure of the kind of
support he would get from cabinet, he had no problem leaning
on Smallwood to persuade those same cabinet ministers to vote
him a substantial increase in salary. In a series of four notes
under cover of the December 12, 1950 letter, where he proposed
the $45 million paper mill, Valdmanis also detailed his plans for
the cement mill, "our proposed big development corporation"
and other industries to help round out a program of economic
development. By his own modest admission, this plan was the
"minimum needed" for the future development of the province.
Included in the same note was a salary request, that if approved,
would increase Valdmanis' pay from a "try-out" level of "714
dollars per month" to $2,080 per month.

Valdmanis must have decided this was the time to go for
broke. He launched a move to consolidate his control over the
government's economic development office, with the proposi-
tion that he have authority to select, hire and fire employees. He
proposed putting all employees on contract, therefore taking
them outside Civil Service Regulations. Valdmanis himself
would determine all salaries, and he undertook to return to the
government, the annual cost of running the Office of the Director General, from the profits generated by the industries.[50]

To boost his campaign for a substantial salary increase and
for total control of the development office, Valdmanis turned to
what may have been a strong dose of fabrication. He related
being "almost heart-broken", since "my personal needs combined with a very advantageous American offer to me ($50,000
a year according to Valdmanis) make my remaining with you in
Newfoundland almost impossible."[51] Valdmanis noted he
would be happy to stay with the Newfoundland government
for half that amount. He had a positive response from Smallwood within a week and it improved his spirits considerably, as
was evident in a subsequent letter to the Premier. Valdmanis
wrote being "happy since you told me that I may count not only
upon your own, but also upon your Cabinet's confidence and
support".[52] Valdmanis had reason to be happy; he had a new

50 Ibid, Note #1, p. 4
51 Ibid, Letter
52 Ibid

four year contract carrying an annual salary of $25,000, three times a cabinet minister's salary.

Much of the internal government debate during this period was devoted to how the new industries would be funded. While the first three industries (cement, gypsum and hardwoods) were funded directly out of the surplus, the government attempted to find another way to finance the balance of its industrialization scheme. As early as the summer of 1951, Valdmanis wrote financiers and floated the idea of raising private capital to fund the new industries.[53] He similarly suggested to a Swiss financier a few months later, "...I would not reject without careful consideration, even a direct loan to the Province (some 20 million dollars)..."[54] Valdmanis continued this line of inquiry into the next year. In a letter to a German banker in March 1952, he noted it was necessary to "consolidate the Province's financial position, and find some good international bank through which our new industries....will be financed...."[55] Valdmanis further wrote he contemplated financing the European industries "on the strength of a Newfoundland guarantee and not through a direct cash advance from the Newfoundland treasury".[56] These inquiries may have underlined a basic conflict in the Cabinet, prompted perhaps by a dwindling surplus as the financial commitment to new industries grew. Valdmanis acknowledged as much in one of his letters, noting "Premier Smallwood...insists...the 19,000,000 dollars, [surplus as of August 17, 1951] except, perhaps, for some small reserve, should be used for building roads, schools and hospitals improving the general social welfare of the people."[57]

NATURAL RESOURCE PLANNING

While much of Smallwood's energy during this period was

---

53 Letter, Alfred Valdmanis to Warburg and Company Limited, August 17, 1951, File 6.00.012. JRS Collection
54 Letter, Alfred Valdmanis to Dr. Paul Hagenbach, December 1, 1951, File 6.00.012. JRS Collection
55 Letter, Alfred Valdmanis to Dr. W. Hinneberg, March 3, 1952, File 6.00.022. JRS Collection
56 Ibid
57 Letter, Valdmanis to Warburg and Company, August 17, 1951

devoted to the industrialization program, the government also
paid attention to the potential of natural resource development.
Labrador was especially seen as a promising source of resource
wealth. Smallwood had long viewed resource development as a
key to becoming "a self-supporting Province, independent and
proud."[58] Recounting to the legislature the potential of mineral
development in the province in the early days of Confederation,
Smallwood remarked,

> When you look at the iron mines of Bell Island, the fluor-
> spar [sic] mines at St. Lawrence, and above all, at the
> fantastic iron mines in Labrador, you cannot help wonder-
> ing if these are all, and whether indeed, the mineral wealth
> of Newfoundland, including Labrador, may not yet be
> enough to make us known as the new Alaska of North
> America.[59]

In late 1950, Valdmanis recalled in a note to Smallwood how
they had earlier proposed creating a resource development
corporation funded 95% by the Newfoundland government
and 5% by private interests in New York. That scheme contemplated giving "50% or even more, of the company's profits" to
the New York concern.[60] The plan had been worked out by
Smallwood and Valdmanis on a train ride from St. John's to
Corner Brook. Valdmanis claimed in late 1950 the plan had now
been "improved", and that "the discrepancy between investment and the right to profits is wiped out."[61] Under the new
plan, he stated, the government and the New York people
would "participate on equal terms", meaning they would
"share the profits, if any, in proportion to the shares owned" and
that in any event, the Newfoundland government would own
51% of the shares.[62]

The New York negotiations, which had kept Valdmanis in
the United States for at least a month, were to have been concluded with a signing by Smallwood and Attorney General Les
Curtis around January 8, 1951. It was clear however from a letter

58 Proceedings, July 19, 1949, p. 50
59 Ibid
60 Letter, Valdmanis to Smallwood, December 12, 1950. Note #2, p. 1
61 Ibid, p. 2
62 Ibid

Valdmanis wrote to a friend at the MIAG company in Germany later in January, that negotiations were not going as expected. The signing was delayed until the week of February 6 in St. John's. That in turn, delayed a trip Valdmanis had planned to make to Germany. The investors in the proposed Newfoundland and Labrador Corporation would be "Wallstreet bankers, Canadian investment bankers and the Newfoundland Government itself.[63]

By this period, several facets of the economic development plan were in place. Key for Smallwood, Alfred Valdmanis was now in charge of the program. And while the government talked optimistically of funding development through bond issues and its development corporation, the only readily available source of money appeared to be the surplus accumulated by Commission of Government. It was to that fund that Smallwood and Valdmanis would turn to finance their program.

---

63 Letter, Valdmanis to Smallwood, January 27, 1951, File 6.00.022. JRS Collection

2

The Policy Takes Shape

From the outside, Smallwood offered a cautious and prudent approach to economic development. Inside the government though, it was a different story as the cabinet moved quickly to approve new industries for Newfoundland. The March 10, 1952 cabinet meeting exemplified this. In it, Rudolf Hanhart and Gustav Carl Weis presented their proposal for a new pressboard industry in Newfoundland. Immediately after their presentation, the two industrialists, along with Edward Wyss, a director of the Swiss People's Bank and Newfoundland's Director General of Economic Development, Alfred Valdmanis, left the cabinet meeting. Inside the cabinet room, Smallwood and the cabinet gave quick approval to the proposal and instructed the Attorney-General, Les Curtis, to draft an agreement. This was followed in short order by a decision to enable the Premier and Minister of Economic Development to complete an agreement with Hanhart and Associates "involving assistance by way of a government loan and/or guarantee of bonds, to a value of $575,000...."[1]

Later that meeting, a draft agreement was prepared for Smallwood's signature. Newfoundland had another industry. This was typical of the break-neck speed with which Smallwood and Valdmanis were industrializing Newfoundland.

Harold Horwood (Liberal MHA for Labrador, 1949-51) writes in his biography of Smallwood, that while "many of Joey's friends and closest associates disliked and distrusted Dr. Valdmanis from the moment they first met him", Smallwood

---

1 Certified Cabinet Minutes, March 10, 1952. Minutes 251-'52; 252-'52; and 253-'52. File 2.03.004. JRS Collection

19

himself was unaffected by their opinion.[2] According to Horwood, within months of Valdmanis' hiring in 1950, Smallwood and Valdmanis had become "the real rulers of Newfoundland."[3]

Smallwood and Valdmanis were a dynamic pair, setting off with either the Finance Minister Greg Power or Attorney General Les Curtis in tow. The trips were nearly always to Europe, where Smallwood was fond of saying, he was "fishing in troubled waters". Smallwood explained his strategy in a 1951 speech to a Boston audience that he was courting for capital in order to develop the province's mineral wealth, timber stands and water power.

> You need only see once the fantastic devastation of Hamburg, Cologne, Dusseldorf, Frankfurt and Munich and a hundred other industrial cities of Germany to understand why so many industrialists on the continent of Europe are anxious to pull out and establish themselves on this side of the water. They have no dollars, it's true, but the Newfoundland Government happens to have some millions of spare dollars, so I have visited many of these industrialists with my personal invitation to accept loans from the Newfoundland Government if they will bring industrial plants to Newfoundland.[4]

While it may be true that Smallwood had a vision for the development of Newfoundland, he appeared to be without any kind of plan or comprehensive strategy. Apart from the obvious goal of creating jobs, there was no underlying philosophy. This was evident in Smallwood's remarks when he announced a machinery plant for Octagon, near St. John's in July 1951. In what appeared to be a simplistic justification, he told the crowd "developed countries manufacture machinery" and "any country who [sic] does this is industrial."[5]

Prior to establishing the first industries, Smallwood reported to the press on a trip to the industrial section of West

---

2 Horwood, p. 173
3 Ibid, p, 173
4 Speech, given at Boston, Massachusetts, October 15, 1951. File 7.02.004. JRS Collection
5 *Evening Telegram*, July 14, 1951

Germany in which he covered 2200 miles by car. "We are working energetically on five new industries that will give about 4,000 full-time and part-time jobs" he boasted, adding his target was 10,000 new jobs in the coming two or three years.[6]

An even more ambitious undertaking was outlined a year later in October 1951, after Smallwood, Curtis and Valdmanis returned to Newfoundland from a six-week trip to Europe. In a province-wide broadcast, Smallwood described his commitment to economic development and then disclosed he had just committed the government to fifteen new industries for Newfoundland.

> The 15 new industries will give at least 3,000 new full-time jobs before the end of next year, and another 2,000 before the end of two years from now. Those fifteen new industries, along with the eight new industries we had up to six weeks ago, will give nearly 6,000 new full-time jobs by the end of next year, and about 15,000 jobs before the end of two years.[7]

Not all those industries would be established. But Smallwood's comments made it clear the government would continue the program announced the year before, when he established the cement and gypsum plants at Corner Brook, and the hardwoods plant at Donovan's, near St. John's.

The cement plant at Corner Brook was designed to produce 100,000 tons a year and expected by the government to create more than one million dollars a year in profit.[8] The plant had a natural advantage over firms attempting to import cement - it had access to abundant local supplies of limestone and shale, necessary ingredients in the manufacture of portland cement. In addition, Corner Brook had a rail link with the rest of the island, an important consideration given the problems associated with transporting a commodity as heavy as cement. The government and the plant's managers also counted on being informed about federal housing tenders in the Maritime Region, so they could

---

6 *Evening Telegram*, October 28, 1950
7 Smallwood Speech broadcast on October 12, 1951. File 7.02.004. JRS Collection.
8 Letter, Alfred Valdmanis to Warburg and Company, London. August 17, 1951.
   Valdmanis Memoranda, "Banking Houses" File 6.00.012. JRS Collection

bid on Central Mortgage and Housing contracts.[9] It was evident early on however, that the cost estimates for constructing the cement plant were badly out of line. Cabinet was asked by the German construction company, MIAG, to add an additional $523,180 (US) to the contract to cover increased labour and material costs "which had increased in the period between the estimates and the delivery of the equipment for the Cement Mill."[10] Cabinet had its own officials undertake an investigation of MIAG's claim and was advised to settle it for half the amount, which it did on December 3, 1951.[11] Twelve days later, a fuller account of the underestimation of the cement plant costs was revealed, when cabinet approved a supplementary cost of $820,000, bringing the final bill to $3,700,000.[12] That the final cost was significantly higher than the original estimate, should not have come as a surprise, at least not to Smallwood. Valdmanis had written the Premier from Germany six months earlier informing him "MIAG will suffer a net loss of at least ½ million dollars."[13]

In the same letter, Valdmanis reported he had met with Benno Schilde, the contractor for the gypsum plant at Corner Brook. They too were running over on their costs. Valdmanis conveyed to Smallwood "their [Benno Schilde's] great worries...where they are afraid they are going to lose a considerable amount of money."[14] Three years later, Valdmanis would be charged and convicted of extorting bribes of $270,000 from MIAG and $200,000 from Benno Schilde. A bribe of that magnitude from MIAG may partly explain their large claim against the government for increased costs associated with construction of the cement plant at Corner Brook.

Like the cement plant, the gypsum plant at Corner Brook

9   Memo, A.L. Graudins, Nfld. Economic Development Department to Alfred
     Valdmanis, Director General of Economic Development, October 10, 1952. File
     6.00.023. JRS Collection.
10 Minute in Council, December 3, 1951, Certified Cabinet Minutes. File 2.03.003.
     JRS Collection.
11 Ibid
12 Minute in Council, 1072-'51, Department of Economic Development 31-'51 and
     34-'51, December 15, 1951. File 2.03.003. JRS Collection.
13 Letter, Valdmais to Smallwood, May 16, 1951. File 6.00.006. JRS Collection.
14 Ibid

was also intended to take advantage of local natural resources (gypsum from the Flat Bay area) in the manufacture of plaster-board for the local housing and building industry. The plant was to be financed outright by the government and sold once it was in operation. The cement and hardwoods plants were also financed in this way, and were part of the government's strategy "to build the plants using Newfoundland's surplus, sell them, and then build others with the proceeds of the previous sales, and so on ad infinitum."[15] Valdmanis was of the view though, that the cement plant might constitute an exception to the general policy.

> As the cement mill is vital to every future industrial devel-
> opment plan of Mr. Smallwood's Government, he may
> make an exception in this case, and, in deviation from his
> strict general policy of sticking to private enterprise, he
> may decide to establish a crown company to keep and
> operate the mill.[16]

Smallwood predicted the cement plant would create 200 jobs while the gypsum plant would provide employment for 300 people.

Jobs were also a significant factor in the third industry that was launched in 1951 —the hardwoods or birch veneer and plywood plant at Donovan's. The plant, estimated to cost $1,300,000, ended up costing the government $2 million. 250 people were expected to be employed at the plant with hun-dreds more workers in the woods.

The hardwoods plant was intended to use Newfoundland birch and imported woods, such as mahogany from the Ivory Coast. Its main products would be birch veneer, doors, flooring and plywood.[17] The build-up to the opening of the mill was typical of the approach with all the industries Smallwood started under the industrialization program. The program boasted jobs, implied a fixed cost, foresaw no problems and predicted profits from operation. Newfoundland Hardwoods was handed over to businessman Chester Dawe to operate. To

---

15 Horwood, p. 171
16 Letter, Valdmanis to Warburg and Company, London. August 17, 1951
17 *Financial Post*, June 2, 1951. Volume 45, p. 49

secure a woods supply, the company was given control over all
the birch stands on Crown Lands and was extended permission
to cut birch on lands owned by the two paper companies. The
mood surrounding the establishment of the company was
euphoric. The *Financial Post* concluded in June 1951:

> No difficulty is anticipated in selling the product, rather
> the expected trouble is keeping up with orders.[18]

Valdmanis predicted the company would return a half
million dollars a year in profit to the government.[19]

Despite all the public assurances of success for Newfoundland Hardwoods, there was sufficient concern about the company in the first year of operation, for government to establish a
sub-committee of cabinet (consisting of the Premier, the Attorney-General, and the Ministers of Public Works, Health, Supply
and Finance). The committee was "to examine into the admini-
stration of Newfoundland Hardwoods Limited and report to
the Executive Council as to what, if any measures should be
taken to improve the efficiency and economy of its operations."[20] The plant got off to an inauspicious start, experiencing
a strike in its first year and the replacement of its technical
manager.[21]

In late May 1952, three months after the cabinet sub-committee was formed, the government again took a special interest
in Newfoundland Hardwoods. The cabinet authorized the acting Minister of Economic Development (the Minister of Public
Works) "to implement any decision with regard to temporary
financing required by Newfoundland Hardwoods Ltd."[22]

During the period when cabinet appeared to be preoccu-
pied with the problems at Newfoundland Hardwoods, it
authorized a $575,000 loan for a related company to manufac-
ture pressboard. Atlantic Hardboard Industries Limited would
be built adjacent to the Newfoundland Hardwoods Plant at
Donovan's, using waste wood from the hardwoods plant. At-

---

18 Ibid
19 Letter, Valdmanis to Warburg and Company. August 17, 1951
20 Minute in Council 175-'52, February 2, 1952. File 2.03.004. JRS Collection.
21 Memo, Graudins to Valdmanis, October 10, 1952
22 Minute in Council 541-'52, May 31, 1952. File 2.03.004. JRS Collection.

lantic Hardboard contemplated 100 jobs in the manufacture of a
wall and underlay pressboard comprised of wood shavings and
glue.

From its earliest days however, the second plant had problems with the high moisture content of its wood supply, compel-
ling the Board of Directors in early 1955 to consider asking
government for more money so it could stockpile wood. The
only other option was to add more drying capacity to the plant.
Either decision would require capital Atlantic Hardboard did
not have.[23]

Atlantic Hardboard was a prime example of the speed with
which the new industries were approved by the government. In
an August 1951 letter to a London banking house, Valdmanis
outlined in detail the government's plans for future industrial
development. There was no mention of the pressboard plant,
yet just six months later, cabinet gave approval to finance the
plant.

It is also apparent from Valdmanis' letter on that occasion,
the government remained uncertain about how to raise funds
for the new industries. Valdmanis pointed out that while government would put up 50% of the capital required for industries
after the first three (cement, gypsum and hardwoods plants),
there was no decision on whether this should be in the form of a
guarantee or a direct cash loan from the government.[24] Valdmanis went on to chart several other industries that would be
put in place over the next year, including a leather tannery, a fine
leather goods company, a fur dressing and dyeing plant and
cotton mills. The fur dressing and dyeing factory did not make
it past the idea stage, but the other plants were built, at an initial
cost of about $5 million to the government. Between them, the
new plants were expected to result in more than 1000 direct
jobs.[25]

The construction of these industries and the Atlantic Hard-

23 Minutes, Board of Directors Meetings, Atlantic Hardboards Industries Limited,
   February 9, 1955. File 3.08.139. JRS Collection.
24 Letter, Valdmanis to Warburg and Company
25 Letter, Gordon Pushie, Department of Economic Development, to Canadian
   Machinery and Maunufacturing News, November 18, 1952. File 6.00.023. JRS
   Collection.

board plant represented a departure in policy from the manner in which the first three industries were financed. Instead of financing industries outright, the government's policy now was to finance half the capital requirements of new industry. While the government's half would be in cash, private investment could be in the form of "know-how, machinery, any other material, engineering supervision, erection, building, etc."[26]

One of the first plants to be built under the new financing scheme was a tannery at Carbonear in 1952. The private investor involved in this project was Wilhelm Dorn, a Czechoslovkian-born, German citizen, whose family went back three generations in the tannery business. The initial promise was for 150 jobs with an increase to 200. However, after nearly four years of operation, only 21 people were employed. The plant tanned only 100 hides a day, far short of its objective of 150. An important signal of the problems faced by the company was evident in a report Wilhelm Dorn gave the Board in February 1956. He reported an order for Maxine Footwear Limited (the government had provided a $58,000 loan eight months earlier to acquire raw materials to fill the order) was cancelled "due to delays in delivery of both raw materials and the finished product,..."[27]

The summer of 1951 brought one of the biggest commitments yet of government capital to the industrial development program. In July, Smallwood announced a $5 million machine factory to be known as Canadian Machinery and Industry Construction Limited. The plant was constructed at Octagon by MIAG, the same firm that built the cement plant at Corner Brook. *The Evening Telegram* gave an account of the announcement.

> They will manufacture all kinds of machinery...Plans are to proceed by several stages. They will start with the construction of a very sizeable manufacturing plant to be enlarged in several steps in a short period of time...Milling, grinding, crushing and drilling machines will be made. As

---

26 Letter, Valdmanis to Smallwood, May 11, 1951. File 3.08.004. JRS Collection
27 Minutes, Board of Directors Meeting of Newfoundland Tanneries (Wm. Dorn) Ltd., February 15, 1956. File 3.08.001, JRS Collection.

the factory expands, bigger machines will be included in the produce of the factory.[28]

The paper reported "initial employment for the factory will be 500 men", with the promise of more to be added as the factory was enlarged. The government was even more boastful in the Speech from the Throne in October 1951, a month before Small-wood called a snap election. The speech bragged the machinery plant "seems likely to become perhaps the biggest labour-giving enterprise in Newfoundland, apart from the fisheries."[29]

The promise in July 1951 of hundreds of immediate jobs — and up to 5000 jobs eventually from the machinery plant — was followed a month later by an announcement that a textile plant — United Cotton Mills — would be built at St. John's. Predicting work for 800 people, Smallwood said the government would put up a $2 million, 10-year loan toward the $4 million dollar cost of the project. The plans called for raw material to be imported from Turkey, Iran, Haiti and the United States, woven into cotton cloth and then made into products such as "skirts, dresses, table cloths, service uniforms and such."[30] Six years later, the promise of 800 jobs seemed like a cruel joke, as fewer than 100 people were employed at the textile plant.[31]

The government's investment in the new industries was now over $13 million, greater than half of the pre-Confederation surplus that was available for economic development, including school and road construction. Despite Smallwood's public statements from as early as March 1951, that the government would no longer help finance new industries,[32] the $4.5 million invested in the machinery plant and the two textile mills, was proof the government-sponsored industrialization program was still in high gear.

---

28 *The Evening Telegram*, July 14, 1951 p.3
29 Speech from the Throne, October 25, 1951. Proceedings of the House of Assembly. p.55
30 *The Evening Telegram*, August 10, 1951, p. 3
31 Michael F. Harrington, "New and Old Industries in an Old Colony — A Review of Newfoundland's Industrial Revolution", *Atlantic Advocate*, September 1957, Vol. 48(1), p. 19
32 *The Evening Telegram*, March 10, 1951, "Government Backs $1,000,000 Plant to Manufacture Pressboard" and Letter, Valdmanis to Warburg, August 17, 1951.

JOBS

There appears to have been some confusion during this period about the potential for jobs as a result of the new industries. Smallwood predicted in late 1951 the entire industrial development program would bring "15,000 new jobs before the end of two years from now."[33] A senior civil servant wrote a year later, "the goal with this program is 10,000 new jobs."[34] (The difference may be explained by Smallwood's inclusion of the promise of 5,000 jobs at the machinery plant at Octagon.) Clearly, neither the job estimates nor the talked-about embargo on government financing of new industries seemed particularly relevant, as it appeared the program had its own momentum under Smallwood's and Valdmanis' leadership.

Smallwood and Valdmanis were an impressive tag-team, travelling throughout Europe in an effort to diversify an economy that was over-reliant on the resource sector. They were neither deterred by criticism from the floor of the House of Assembly nor by admonishments from the editorial page of The *Evening Telegram*, which reminded the government "the finances of Newfoundland are by no means inexhaustible" and "apart from Mr. Smallwood himself, no one has the slightest conception...where the markets are, or what may be the cost of transporting to these markets."[35] That was a relevant point, considering that many of the industries were premised on strong export sales. But Smallwood was unconcerned about criticism and his march toward industrialization seemed unstoppable.

The late fall of 1951 brought a general election and the first test for Smallwood and his government's policies. The *Evening Telegram*'s editor might have found fault, but voters apparently found little to reprimand the government about, returning Smallwood with twenty-three seats to five for the Conservatives.

During 1952, the government continued to support new manufacturing ventures. It put $325,000 toward the construc-

33 *Evening Telegram*, October 13, 1951, p. 3
34 Letter, Gordon Pushie, Economic Development Department to Kent Strong, Canadian Dow Jones Limited. File 6.00.023, JRS Collection.
35 *Evening Telegram* editorial, "Give Newfoundland the Facts", October 16, 1951

tion of the Hanning Electric Limited battery plant at Topsail, promising 100 jobs in the bargain. By mid-1954, a familiar, yet sad story was repeating itself. With six months' production under its belt, the battery plant employed only 17 people. Although the company expected the payroll to soon climb to 30, it anticipated problems reaching peak production of 60,000 automobile batteries, given that Newfoundland used only 12,000 batteries a year.[36] The company appeared to believe the problem reaching peak battery production was a long-term one, indicating it planned to use some of its capacity to turn out plastic products such as drinking cups and brushes.[37]

On the day the government concluded the agreement to build the battery plant, it put up $1 million for construction of a rubber products manufacturing plant at Holyrood. Premised on what was believed to be a ready market for rubber clothes and boots in the Newfoundland fishing industry, the plant was expected to employ 400 people. Undercapitalized, and operating with machinery that some claimed was part of United States aid to Germany under the Marshall Plan, Superior Rubber, as the company was known, lurched from crisis to crisis. In an obvious clampdown on the German managers of the firm, the company's Board decided in late September 1954 that "...no monies were to be advanced for payment of salaries to persons not resident in Newfoundland and not actively engaged in the operation of the plant."[38] A further clampdown was imposed in May 1955, when the Board ordered that no one in the plant had authority to hire staff or sign documents without prior board approval.[39] In the same meeting, all the German employees at the plant, including the manager, were fired.

Smallwood and Valdmanis did not allow themselves many idle moments. Three years after St. John's got its first textile plant under the industrialization program, a second, Terra Nova Textiles, was announced. The announcement was made on July 19, 1954. This plant was to produce mainly work clothes,

36 *Financial Post*, July 3, 1954. Vol. 48. pp.20-26
37 Ibid
38 Minutes, Board of Directors Meeting, Superior Rubber Company Limited, September 27, 1954. File 3.08.184. JRS Collection
39 Minutes, Superior Rubber, May 12, 1955

especially coveralls. Expected to employ about 120 people, the company was one of the few begun under the government plan to come close to meeting its employment target.

THE CONCEPTION BAY INDUSTRIES

More industries were soon to make an appearance, centred on the north shore of Conception Bay. Atlantic Gloves Limited was built at Carbonear with the assistance of a $350,000 government loan and Gold Sail Leather Goods was established at Harbour Grace. Both plants were examples of downstream processing, utilizing leather produced at the Carbonear tannery operated by Wilhelm Dorn.

Atlantic Gloves represented a departure from the government's standard policy of providing half the start-up capital for the new industries in the form of a guaranteed loan. In the case of Atlantic Gloves, the government put up nearly 65-percent. Smallwood said the decision to vary the rules was made after the owner could not come up the required half of the start-up cost, and rather than lose the industry, the government "came to the conclusion that this industry was so sound in its prospects, so promising in its prospects....we ought to stretch our formula to the extent shown in the agreement now before the House."[40] The company produced what was described as an excellent quality ballet slipper, as well as gloves made of both gazelle skin and sheepskin. The company was hampered, though, by high production costs and stiff competition from external producers.

Gold Sail Leather Goods produced women's handbags, wallets and other leather accessories. Like many of the industries, Gold Sail's market potential in Newfoundland was limited, forcing the company to export if it was to even have a chance at making money. This constituted a problem however, given the intense competition in those markets and the fact that its products were considered to be "high-priced".[41] Gold Sail though, like Atlantic Gloves, came on the highest recommendation from Smallwood. On one of his earliest efforts to explain to the House why the government had guaranteed extra capital to the new industries (including Gold Sail), Smallwood said "they

---

40 Proceedings, March 19, 1953, p.80
41 *Financial Post*, July 3, 1954. Vol.48, p. 26

are making leather goods beyond comparison in North America."[42] Smallwood explained how on a visit to a trade fair in Germany he met the man he had chosen to head up Gold Sail - Anton Schaefers. Smallwood told the House "there was no question about who was boss of that fair. It was the same man Schaefers." Despite being impressed with Schaefers, Smallwood gave the impression the government had driven a hard bargain, saying "it was not until last year that they were able to meet our conditions..."[43]

The northern part of Conception Bay was a favoured location for three more of the new industries. Koch Shoes Limited was established in May 1954 at Harbour Grace with a $750,000 government guarantee; A. Adler Company at Bay Roberts in 1956 with a $550,000 guarantee; and Eckhardt Knitting Mills Limited at Brigus in 1957 with a $387,400 guarantee.

Smallwood produced glowing reports of the products that emerged from the new industries. About Koch Shoes, he told the legislature "they are turning out footwear over there that is going to be a good seller...."[44]. Smallwood predicted Eckhardt Mills would sell its lower-priced products "in every nook and cranny of Newfoundland", while "I prophesy that their high-class products will sell all across Canada and the United States."[45] The Premier was equally proud of the fact he had persuaded the English chocolate maker, A. Adler, to disassemble its chocolate factory in Britain and ship it to Newfoundland. In a 1956 debate on Conservative William Browne's motion for a Royal Commission into the government's industrial policy, Smallwood had the page deliver an Adler's bar to opposition leader Malcolm Hollett and invited him to sample "the flavour and goodness" of a bar "made by one of England's greatest firms, now in Bay Roberts."[46]

Yet, all those glowing reports from Smallwood could not solve a basic problem faced by the three plants. They all had difficulty competing outside Newfoundland. While Koch Shoes

42 Proceedings, June 7, 1954, p. 1471
43 Ibid, p. 1472
44 Proceedings, June 7, 1954, p. 1471
45 Ibid, p. 1473
46 Proceedings, March 28, 1955, p. 97

was assisted by several contracts to supply footwear to the Canadian military, the chocolate and knitwear companies were left to fend for themselves in a crowded and distant North American marketplace.

The industries were encouraged through a government loan guarantee program that was flexible, generous and forgiving. These characteristics of the loan guarantee program were obvious in the cabinet decision to extend better than 50-50 terms "in exceptional cases, where circumstances justify a departure from established practice."[47] This flexibility accommodated the establishment of Atlantic Gloves in Carbonear. The generous and forgiving nature of the program would be proven many times over, as will be demonstrated in the next chapter.

There is no evidence during his tenure as Director General of Economic Development from 1950-1953, that anyone other than Valdmanis and his cadre of employees, had a role in overseeing the new industries. Typically, Valdmanis studied proposals and negotiated general terms for the new industries, to be followed by a visit with the principals from Smallwood and one or two senior ministers. Subsequent to these encounters, the investors were typically invited back to Newfoundland to make their pitch to the entire cabinet. Shortly after, sometimes in the same cabinet meeting, approval and financial support would be given to a new industry. The available evidence is mute on what, if any independent studies were undertaken to support these decisions. Indeed, the only references to studies come in mid-1956. With many of the industries in trouble, the government contracted the Arthur D. Little Company from Boston to assess 13 of the 16 industries, in Smallwood's words, to "take stock of these new industries". He told the House some were in "a very healthy position", while others "need nothing more than an improvement in management" and still others "whose position and prospects upon careful analysis may prove to be discouraging."[48]

Prior to this time, the government shed little light on the new industries. Smallwood generally did the talking and that

47 Minute in Council 117-'52, February 2, 1952. File 2.03.004. JRS Collection
48 *Financial Post*, June 29, 1957. Vol.51. pp. 59-60

was usually reserved for the annual trip to the House to approve loans and loan guarantees approved by the cabinet in the previous year. Any doubt Smallwood raised about the new industries was immediately followed by a story of a miraculous recovery. Speaking about the tannery at Carbonear in a 1956 speech, the Premier said for the previous two or three years, it was the industry "I thought had the least chance of succeeding..." Then he continued, "...out of the clear sky, not one, but several miracles occurred." Those miracles, Smallwood told the House, were from hockey skate makers and "great boot and shoe manufacturers" for more than one million square feet of leather. He concluded Wilhelm Dorn "has hit pay dirt, gold".[49]

Smallwood did the same kind of rhetorical dance about Atlantic Hardboard, which, while "formed...with typical German thoroughness" was "shot to pieces with one little factor which they had never taken into account, namely that wood in Newfoundland...contained a high degree of moisture."[50] Smallwood made the case for a loan to cover the cost of an additional wood dryer for the plant, as well as the need for a warehouse and some chipping machines. When asked a sticky question by the Opposition if any of the $300,000 loan would cover running expenses for the plant, Smallwood replied "not at all" and moved on to talk about the cement plant, saying "we have no concerns with the running expenses of North Star Cement."[51]

Only rarely did Smallwood lapse into anything resembling an admission of failure or near-failure with respect to the new industries. One such occasion where he did allow some doubt was in a speech in the late winter of 1953 when Smallwood advised caution about the estimate of 150 jobs at Atlantic Gloves: "I have had enough experience with these new industries to suggest that the number to be employed had better be given with some restraint."[52] By the mid-1950's, four years after the industrialization program began, questions were asked in many quarters about the status of the new industries. The annual request to the House to approve supplementary funding

---

49 Proceedings, March 28, 1956. p. 105
50 Proceedings, June 7, 1954, p. 1474
51 Ibid, p. 1475
52 Speech to House of Assembly, 1951. File 7.02.004. JRS Collection

for the industries made it increasingly difficult to hide the real goings-on and the reasons for the loans. William Browne wrote in his book: "In 1955, the general feeling in St. John's was that the policy was a failure."[53] Smallwood was unwilling to concede his plan was not working. In rejecting Browne's request for a Royal Commission, he replied, "I see no reason..." and concluded about the industries, "most of them are doing very well indeed."[54]

Smallwood's rosy comments about the industries were set against newspaper reports that painted a gloomy picture for several of the industries (the *Financial Post* in particular wrote several articles spelling out problems the industries faced) and against allegations that some of the plants were poorly run. Available information suggests the government withheld the true status of many of the industries for several years, arguing in public everything was fine, while in private, there was outright acknowledgement that many of the industries were encountering serious problems.

A *Financial Post* survey of the industries in July 1954 revealed the firms faced a bevy of serious problems. Its findings ran counter to Smallwood's earlier rhetoric that "...these industries...[will] manufacture things for sale in Newfoundland, and all parts of Canada, in the United States, and in all parts of the world."[55] By 1954, the new firms were facing the reality of competing with companies already well established in Canada and the United States. The newspaper outlined several problems: high transportation costs; the cost of importing raw materials; and a shortage of skilled labour. The Canadian Machinery and Industry Construction Limited (CMIC) at Octagon was to have become a major Canadian producer of heavy industrial machinery, but it discovered "bringing in raw materials and shipping out finished products to distant points is a costly procedure."[56] The company was also finding that even in the local Newfoundland market, "mainland firms with large-scale

---

53 William J. Browne. Eight-Four Years a Newfoundlander (St. John's: Dicks and
     Company, Limited) 1981 p.130
54 Proceedings, March 28, 1956. p. 97
55 Smallwood Speech, October 12, 1951. File 7.02.004. JRS Collection
56 *Financial Post*, July 3, 1954. Vol.48. pp.20-26

production could undersell a local producer in many lines."[57] The paper reported the same kinds of problems were being experienced at the cement, gypsum and rubber plants.

The rubber products plant in particular came in for a lot of critical attention. Conservative MHA William Browne reported being told the product manufactured by the plant was "inferior". Browne had a copy of an affidavit from Frank Pronold, a senior member of Superior's management, who made several allegations. Pronold claimed the company was steadily losing money; that the rubber footwear produced by the plant was defective; that the plant was badly constructed; and that it was using second-hand machinery, some of it stamped "Marshall Plan". Pronold's recipe for righting the plant's problems was to close the plant "at once for a period of four weeks for a complete re-organization from the top down."[58] Browne wrote that Smallwood's response to the allegations was "it is not worth the paper it is written on." He concluded Smallwood was going "to brazen it out."[59] Three months after these events though, the Board of Superior Rubber had obviously decided there was enough concern about the operation of the company that it fired the German management team.

The Conservative leader, John Higgins, likened the government's spending on the new industries to the pied piper: "Our pied pipers did not pipe away the children of Newfoundland, but in excellent order, they have managed to pipe many dollars down the drain in a good many instances."[60] Three years later, another Conservative leader, Malcolm Hollett, in debate on more loans for the new industries, told the government the opposition was "a bit concerned about bringing in a loan bill every year practically for the last four or five years" and that with the pre-Confederation surplus gone, "we must know that there is a limit to the borrowing capacity of this Province."[61]

While the government carried on bravely in public about the industries, privately, there were signs of trouble. A memo

---

57 Ibid
58 Browne, p. 128
59 Browne, p. 129
60 Proceedings, March 19, 1953, p. 81
61 Proceedings, May 4, 1956, p.987

from Smallwood to the Deputy Minister of Economic Development just before Christmas 1953 had a tone of desperation. Upset that government agencies were not buying enough products from the new industries, the Premier wrote bluntly that willingness to buy "shall be regarded as co-operation with the government" and failure to do so would be seen as "non-cooperation." Smallwood termed the existing situation "inexcusable" and "is not to be tolerated."[62]

This general state of concern was set against a backdrop where events were not turning out as planned. While the public statements proclaimed the CMIC plant at Octagon would turn out heavy machinery, memoranda from the company to the cabinet indicated it was not heavy machinery at all that would carry the plant in its early years, but substantial orders from the Defense Department for the manufacture of shells. When the Defence Department rejected that suggestion and the orders failed to materialize, CMIC found itself unable to pay either the principal or interest on its $2.5 million government loan guarantee.[63]

By late 1953, the job of Director General had passed to Gordon Pushie, a Newfoundlander. Valdmanis had moved to Montreal to become chairman of Newfoundland and Labrador Corporation. Pushie not only inherited Valdmanis' old job; he also inherited the problems the industrialization program was beginning to hatch. He cabled Smallwood on the Premier's Christmas vacation in Jamaica in January 1954 about "the desperate financial situation of Newfoundland Hardwoods".[64] A month later, Pushie was writing that he was "concerned" about the financial position of Superior Rubber Company Limited.[65]

By now, enough seeds of doubt had been planted in the public's mind about the new industries to temper Smallwood's exaggerated claims about their impact on Newfoundland.

---

62 Letter, Smallwood to Norman Short, December 17, 1953. File 3.08.004. JRS Collection

63 Letter, CMIC to Smallwood, March 28, 1955. File 3.08.058. JRS Collection

64 Cable, Gordon Pushie to Smallwood, January 11, 1954. File 3.08.004. JRS Collection)

65 Letter, Pushie to D.W.K. Dawe, February 8, 1954. File 3.08.004. JRS Collection

3

Problems Aplenty: The Industries
Run Into Trouble

The March 31, 1953 letter from the National Gypsum Company in Buffalo, New York, must have put a chill in Joey Smallwood's bones. Eleven days earlier, National Gypsum had given every indication it would make one of Smallwood's most fervent wishes come true — National had set out a tentative offer to buy the gypsum plant at Corner Brook. A sale would have given credibility to the government's strategy of selling the first three industries. Instead of finalizing the deal though, National was writing to say it had changed its mind. The reasons, arrived at during "careful study" by National Gypsum's management, amounted to a polite but firm indictment of the Corner Brook plant.

While the company considered the plant to be "of good design and construction", it underlined several weaknesses, including the mill's low operating speed — "45 feet per minute" — which "is customary in Europe", but far below speeds obtained in the United States where "our machines average three times that speed."[1] The low operating speed was just one of the reasons National Gypsum cited in the letter to Smallwood. It saw additional weaknesses in the limited year-round market in Newfoundland, which necessitated selling into the mainland market. National viewed the mainland market as fraught with problems because of high transportation and warehousing costs. Although it did not indicate the Newfoundland govern-

---

1 Letter, National Gypsum Company, Buffalo, NY to Joseph Smallwood, March 31, 1953. File 3.08.285. JRS Collection

ment's asking price for the mill, National Gypsum implied it was in the $6 million range. It concluded "our people do not feel that it is advisable.... at the original price that you have suggested for the plant". It said the Corner Brook mill would produce at 40% of what the company could get out of a new $6 million plant.[2]

Rejected by National Gypsum, the government continued to look for a "satisfactory purchaser".[3] But Atlantic Gypsum looked anything like a prime candidate for privatization, a point that was made clear when the company's board of directors was informed of Atlantic's operations in late 1954. Dependent on the mainland market for close to 90-percent of its sales, the board was told of the "almost complete collapse of our sales on the mainland" resulting "in unreasonably high 'frozen in' stocks in our warehouses and in financial losses amounting to hundreds of thousands of dollars."[4]

Atlantic Gypsum's problems on the Canadian mainland began in mid-1954 when mainland competitors increased their production. The competition built new capacity, and as a result, the battle for market share became "increasingly fierce". Atlantic's sole sales agent on the mainland — International Building Products (IBP) of Montreal — advised Corner Brook that despite the increased competition, it did not expect a reduction in the price for gypsum wallboard. Atlantic's executives were therefore taken by surprise on August 13 when mainland gypsum makers dropped their prices by $5 a thousand square feet.[5] Atlantic's sales plunged immediately, leading to "an all time high" stockpile of 12 million square feet, worth about $450,000. Atlantic Gypsum placed the blame for the main share of its problem at the feet of IBP which it complained "have only one man as a sales force in the field and even that one man...is serving not Atlantic Gypsum Limited only...", but also had to sell other lines "which IBP carries".[6] The problems in the main-

2   Ibid
3   Proceedings, May 31, 1954
4   Atlantic Gypsum Limited. "Report on the Status of Our Present Mainland Sales
    Representation", November 15, 1954. File 3.08.024. JRS Collection
5   Ibid
6   Ibid

land market forced Atlantic to close its Corner Brook plant for three weeks at the end of August 1954. When it reopened, operations were reduced from two shifts to one.

The importance of the Canadian market could not be over-stated. Atlantic Gypsum had arrived at the conclusion it was the only reasonably sound export market after a survey of the United States a year-and-a-half earlier. The February 1953 survey concluded "there is no chance of selling our boards in the United States at a price satisfactory to us."[7]

The crisis caused by the price drop in the mainland market left Atlantic in a cash crunch. Without the working capital to meet its losses, Atlantic turned to its 100% owner, the Newfoundland government. Cabinet gave approval in early December 1954 for $135,000 "as prepayment...in respect of aggregate losses of $250,000 for the current year."[8]

The position in which Atlantic Gypsum found itself — with costs exceeding income — would become a familiar refrain for most of the companies financed under the government's industrialization program. This unflattering picture of the new industries was painted consistently in "official" company and government documents. These of course, were kept from the public. The government's public pronouncements were full of hope and predictions of growth. The stated immediate goal of the industrialization program was jobs, with the added advantage of a diversified economy where "cement, gypsum, plasterboard, fibreboard....these are the new commodities that must now be added to the fish and the newsprint paper and the minerals that have constituted the mainstay of Newfoundland's industrial production."[9] While the government, and especially Smallwood proclaimed the new program was working, by virtue of the jobs it created and the wages it paid, the industries were destructing one by one.

---

7   Letter, Ernst Leja, Managing Director of Atlantic Gypsum Company Limited, to Gordon Pushie, Director General of Economic Development, January 26, 1954. File 3.08.024. JRS Collection.
8   Minute-in-Council, December 3, 1954. P.25-'54. File 2.03.006. JRS Collection.
9   Proceedings, May 31, 1954. p. 1149

THE CEMENT PLANT

The cement plant was touted by Valdmanis as a certain profit-maker, even before it had been built. This claim, along with the government's intention to sell the first three plants as early as possible, led to a flurry of activity during the early years of the program. The first set of negotiations took place with the so-called "New York Group". Valdmanis spent six weeks in New York trying to put together a deal that would net the government $1.5 million (US) and an additional $1.2 to $1.5 million Canadian. The negotiations were to build on a memorandum of agreement signed July 19, 1950.[10] That deal fell through however, and for the next several years, the government tried to play matchmaker for a plant that became mired in red ink.

Undeterred by the failure of their first attempt to sell the as yet, untried cement plant to the New York Group, the government pursued other buyers, including a Texas oil millionaire and a Belgian Baron. The dealings with Baron Kronacher began on the heels of the failure of the New York talks. The Baron had diverse holdings — among them, two cement plants in Belgium and a sugar beet factory in Manitoba. He was a friend of powerful Canadian cabinet minister C.D. Howe, and was a member of the Belgian Senate. The Baron was offered the Corner Brook mill for $3 million cash in Canadian dollars up front and another $600,000 to be paid over five years. At the same time as the Baron conducted negotiations with the Newfoundland government, Valdmanis was approached by a Newark, New Jersey attorney on behalf of a Texas oil millionaire, identified as Mr. Rogers. In a memo to Smallwood, Valdmanis appeared ready to determine how much the American was willing to pay, noting he had told the Americans "...the Government would not consider selling the mill at anything less than Four million dollars (U.S. currency)".[11]

The real negotiating was taking place with the Baron how-

---

10 Memorandum of Agreement between Alfred Valdmanis, Director General of Economic Development and "The New York Group", dated July 19, 1950. This memorandum set out the price and terms with respect to the cement plant and was intended not to be a contract but the basis on which a contract would be negotiated. File 3.08.250. JRS Collection

11 Memo, Valdmanis to Smallwood, May 10, 1951. File 3.08.250. JRS Collection

ever, with the government apparently believing the deal was nearly done. There is evidence of this in a letter from Valdmanis to the lawyer for the Texas firm in early July 1951. Valdmanis said he could sell the plant to the Baron and as a result, could not "preserve the mill for you any longer."[12] The Baron, it seemed, knew how to preserve the option on the mill for himself without making a commitment to purchase the company. He did this by carrying out extensive drilling to determine the purity of limestone deposits at the Corner Brook site. The Texas company, now identified as the Lone Star Cement Company, was not put off by the earlier rejection letter from Valdmanis and asked that "...this deal be held for a few months" since there was "reluctance on the part of the Board to increase its current borrowings."[13] Lone Star added a sweetener to its request, saying it would be worth the government's while to wait as "I am sure that they [the government] would be amply compensated by an increase in the price three or four months hence."[14]

What the Newfoundland government did not know was that while the Baron was negotiating with Valdmanis, he had been trying to entice Lone Star to help finance the deal for the cement plant. This was revealed in a letter from Lone Star to Valdmanis in August 1951. Lone Star let the government know that it was felt "...Konacher did not have the money to swing the deal alone."[15] A month later, the Baron, apparently unaware of the communication between Lone Star and the government, notified Smallwood he was bailing out of talks to land the cement mill as there were too many risks associated with taking on the project. Lone Star meanwhile, did not re-enter the picture. For now, the government had given up on selling the plant and had begun looking for a company to operate the facility. In June 1952, it handed over technical and commercial management to Canadian Machinery Holding Trust.

This move was made just before the plant went into production in the spring of 1952. In its first seven months in operation,

---

12 Letter, Valdmanis to Arthur Slavitt, Newark, N.J., July 4, 1951. File 3.08.250. JRS Collection
13 Letter, Slavitt to Valdmanis, August 3, 1951. File 3.08.250. JRS Collection
14 Ibid
15 Letter, Slavitt to Valdmanis, August 8, 1951. File 3.08.250. JRS Collection

the cement plan ran up a loss of $326,536.[16] The loss was substantially less in the next year, but by 1954, the red ink was dripping badly, with losses of more than $433,000 for the year. North Star had also accumulated interest charges of $422,000 on its $4.74 million, 4-percent government loan.[17]

During this same period, the government attempted to sell the second of the original three industries — Atlantic Gypsum Limited, but that bid failed too. It made no effort to put Newfoundland Hardwoods on the market, choosing instead to lease the plant to Newfoundland businessman Chester Dawe.

The ordeal with the first three industries proved to be an unpromising debut for the strategy of building the plants one at a time, selling them, and using the proceeds to start other industries. That state of affairs however, did not stop Smallwood from trumpeting the new industries' "distinguished and valuable contribution" to the Newfoundland economy. But no level of optimism could counter the disastrous results that started showing on the balance sheets of most of the companies. A look inside the operations of the various industries raises serious questions about what, if any contribution, they were making to Newfoundland.

THE RUBBER PLANT

The rubber products plant built at Holyrood was a case in point. Smallwood promoted the plant as an import substitution industry. He foresaw workers at Holyrood producing rubber clothes and boots that would take a significant part of what he estimated was a $2 million dollar-a-year Newfoundland market.[18] And not only that, an exuberant Smallwood told the House one early spring day in 1953, but he believed "...with the latest machinery, with lots of skilled management behind it...we see no reason, as a Government, why such a plant should not succeed..."[19] By succeed, Smallwood explained, he meant the plant would pay back to the government all the principal and

---

16 North Star Cement Financial Statements, 1952. File 3.08.266. JRS Collection
17 Ibid
18 Proceedings, March 27, 1953. p. 272
19 Ibid

interest on its loan, as well as a profit for the owners of the company.[20]

The firm was given the name Superior Rubber Company Limited, a name that would prove to be a touch ironic given some of the later complaints about its products. Superior ran into trouble soon after it opened. One of its first problems was with the long established St. John's shoe merchants — Parker and Monroe. At issue was the sale to Parker and Monroe of some of the company's test-run rubbers at a price Superior's lawyer later claimed was $1.40 a pair. The company accused Parker and Monroe of employing the test-run rubbers as a poor comparison to its regular lines. The lawyer claimed "...we can only assume that your comparison was carried out with the malicious intent of keeping our client's products off the market..."[21] The shoe store conceded one of its salesmen did make a comparison and was now under orders "...such comparisons were not to be made in future."[22] But the company rejected one of Superior's charges — Parker and Monroe claimed it bought the rubbers for $7.40 a pair, more than five times the amount claimed by Superior. By any account, that was a steep price for rubber boots.

The Parker and Monroe incident paled in comparison to what was happening at the futuristic-looking plant at Holyrood. The German managing director of the plant — Max Braun-Wogau — had been ill and away from the plant for several months in 1954. The president, Karl Grube, had been detained in Germany because of problems with currency control authorities. "A very critical situation exists..." was how Gordon Pushie summed it up in a memo to Smallwood.[23] Smallwood was given the bad news — Superior "was without active control for four months", it was producing only 60 pairs of rubber footwear a day and needed another $400,000 of government money.[24]

20 Ibid
21 Letter, Donald Dawe [Lawyer, Superior Rubber Company Limited] to Parker and Monroe, August 3, 1954. File 3.08.177. JRS Collection
22 Letter, Parker and Monroe to Donald Dawe, August 11, 1954. File 3.08.177. JRS Collection
23 Memo, Gordon Pushie to Smallwood, May 7, 1954. File 2.08.085. JRS Collection
24 Ibid

The German management placed much of the blame for the plant's production problems on the local female workers. On one occasion, Braun-Wogau wrote this unflattering assessment:

> The unreliability and lack of initiative and interest on the part of the female labourers are a great handicap. The girls employed in the Plant come and go continuously. We had to trail through the plant 950 persons in order to build up a team of 80 persons.[25]

In that same memo, Braun-Wogau revealed the picture of a company that was bleeding red ink fast, adding that their operations were "hampered by the shortage of funds."[26] In order to add to its working capital, Superior was diverting the $10,000 the government had loaned for a railway siding connection with the CNR track and it was taking $32,149.44 from its capital account (money intended to be the last instalment on a $70,000 machine to be used in the manufacture of non-slip bath mats, insoles and other rubber goods).[27] The money was needed not to pay invoices for some incoming raw materials, rather it was needed "to take care of the backlog of accounts payable."[28]

Superior was sinking deeper into trouble from which it would be difficult to recover. A German architect who was engaged to help design the factory, wrote to the government to say that he had resigned from the position "...rather than be blamed with the architectonic responsibility for what was being planned against my own convictions..."[29]

Concern about the design and condition of the building was at the centre of a complaint from a Canadian worker at the plant, who wrote Smallwood to explain why he was quitting and heading home to Montreal.

> I am embittered over the appealing [sic] condition of the building itself, its equipment, the senseless waste and destruction of material, the hopelessness of a native ever

25 Memo, Max Braun-Wogau to Gordon Pushie, November 11, 1954, File 3.08.171. JRS Collection
26 Ibid
27 Ibid
28 Ibid
29 Letter, Dr. Ing Thormohlen to Gordon Pushie, January 5, 1955. File 3.08.177. JRS Collection

getting a higher job with better pay although their performance is in most cases better than the performance of the so-called experts.[30]

The politics and the management style at Superior might have been tolerable for the government had the plant produced the quality and quantity of rubber goods Smallwood had predicted just two years before. But with up to 40-percent of its production of the key knee and thigh rubber production being sold as seconds, the company was on shaky ground.[31] It was not helped either by reports like the one relayed to Norman Short, the Deputy Minister of Supply, regarding rubber boots that had been shipped to North Labrador Trading Posts.

> These rubbers thigh and knee, are of very poor quality...The 'Superior' rubbers last the fishermen about two weeks...I have had numerous complaints...they are unglued at the soles, the rubber is peeling off and the men must condemn them...The children's rubbers are the same...We have about three dozen pairs on hand...the people know the quality and won't buy.[32]

By the late winter of 1955, with the company still in a tailspin, Max Braun-Wogau made notes of a conversation in which he informed Gordon Pushie that the government loan of $1.4 million would soon be exhausted. The government, through Pushie, appeared to be getting the message about Superior and its managers. Braun-Wogau wrote that Pushie "took note of this information and said it was premature to discuss further steps..."[33]

Pushie was playing for time. He began a search for another company to run the plant, or if the government was especially lucky, a company to buy it outright. He contacted several large

---

30 Letter, Frank Pronold to Smallwood, February 20, 1955. File 3.08.177. JRS Collection.

31 Memo, Braun-Wogau to Pushie, February 23, 1955. File 3.08.177. JRS Collection

32 Letter, Deputy Minister of Supply to Pushie, January 11, 1955. File 3.08.177. JRS Collection.

33 Memo, Braun-Wogau of conversation with Gordon Pushie, February 23, 1955. File 3.08.177. JRS Collection. [Braun-Wogau made extensive notes of conversations with Pushie and sent them in memo form to Pushie, presumably as a record of their conversations.]

rubber concerns, including Dunlop Canada (April 19, 1955); Greengate and Irwell Rubber Company Limited, London (May 16, 1955); and British Tyre and Rubber Company (May 20, 1955). In less than two months, all three companies ruled out any possibility of their setting up in Newfoundland. Pushie then approached the London plastics and rubber manufacturer — P.P. Cow and Company Limited — and asked them to undertake a study of the Superior operation.

Cow's 20-page report showed Superior with $1.4 million in government loans, a $120,000 bank overdraft, and $72,850 owing in interest to the government. The most damning pieces of evidence though, were the sales figures for 1955. The company managed to go over $5000 in sales for just two months, and in one month, sales plummeted to $203.[34] P.P. Cow cited the "lack of commercial experience" of the general manager and emphatically recommended the Works Manager must "...go at the earliest possible moment."[35] They judged much of the plant to be second-hand and claimed the Germans used the government loan to repay themselves for the machinery. The report said the Germans "...showed a complete lack of expertise or interest in developing the Company..." and it stated the obvious, "the Newfoundland Government now find themselves with a large, inadequately equipped factory, running at a loss..."[36]

The plant, which had run up a deficit of $622,337 by late 1955, was on borrowed time. In February 1956, two months after the P.P. Cow report, the government pulled the plug. Smallwood told the House the plant had "...been disastrously bad and has failed."[37]

PROBLEMS AT THE CONCEPTION BAY PLANTS

Nearly all the new industries turned out to be crisis waiting to happen. The leather-based industries in Harbour Grace and Carbonear were prime examples of this. Intended to manufacture products from leather produced at the tannery in Car-

---

34 Report on Superior Rubber Company by P.P. Cow and Company Limited, November 30, 1955. File 3.08.177. JRS Collection
35 Ibid
36 Ibid
37 Proceedings, March 28, 1956. p. 106

bonear, Atlantic Gloves Limited, Koch Shoes and Gold Sail Leather Goods Limited, were seen as complementary to each other. It did not take long however, for this special relationship to deteriorate, and seriously set back the very reason the plants were established.

The early days of the leather industries though, were characterized by good relations all around. A kind of "all for one and one for all" ethos prevailed. This was demonstrated when Gold Sail caught wind of rumours that "a definite possibility exists that the Tannery at Carbonear will cease operations because of insufficient financial assistance...." Gold Sail rushed to the rescue of its commercial cousin, underscoring several reasons for the government to continue financing the nearby tannery, including the fact it could deliver raw material in mere hours, that its prices were lower than competitors, and that it was supplying the exact type of leather Gold Sail wanted.[38]

"The tannery is now in a position to fill major orders...", wrote the owner, Wilhelm Dorn, to Smallwood in February 1953, providing it received $25,000 in working capital.[39] This was the beginning of several such requests. Three months later, Dorn reported two big shoe companies wanted to place orders for leather, thereby necessitating "larger lots of hides, more chemicals and perhaps more workers." He also required an additional $50,000 in working capital.[40] In the summer of 1953 — for the third time that year — Dorn was beating a well-worn path to the door of the Newfoundland Treasury, asking Smallwood for bridge financing of $50,000 until the Tannery could begin selling hides to Koch Shoes.[41] The government was not prepared to advance the money to Dorn, and instead made a quiet proposal to Koch at the shoe factory that it would lend "at once $30-$40,000" to buy leather from the tannery. To sweeten the deal, the government was prepared to make the loan interest free "until such time as your plant would be ready to buy leather and go into the production of shoes."[42]

38 Letter, Gold Sail Leather Goods Limited to Pushie, March 24, 1954. File 3.08.084. JRS Collection
39 Letter, Wilhlem Dorn to Smallwood, February 9, 1953. File 3.08.098. JRS Collection
40 Letter, Dorn to Smallwood, May 9, 1953. 3.08.098. JRS Collection
41 Letter, Dorn to Smallwood, August 13, 1953. File 3.08.098. JRS Collection

That fall, the government accepted the inevitable with respect to the new industries. Knowing most, if not all, were incapable of meeting the interest or the principal on their loans, the government announced that interest payments due in the first and second years could be postponed until the thirteenth and fourteenth years. In the third and fourth years, the new companies would only be required to pay the interest on their government loans. The principal could be delayed until the fifth year.[43]

This generous treatment did not seem to help with production at the tannery. Dorn received complaints from his Montreal agent who had placed a "substantial order" on December 2, 1954 for sole leather. Four weeks later, the panicked agent wrote that if the leather did not arrive in a few days, "I am afraid we will get in trouble". Ten days after that, and nearly six weeks after he placed the order, the agent wrote Dorn "the customer informed me today he can't wait and will buy from another tannery." Word obviously travelled fast in the leather industry, as the same Montreal agent wrote Dorn again in late February 1955. He related comments from a shoe manufacturer who "wouldn't believe me" on hearing the tannery could promise two weeks delivery.

Dorn meanwhile, attributed his problems to the railway, high power rates and the great distances between Newfoundland and mainland markets.[44] He informed the government the only way to correct the problem was to buy a modern warehouse in Montreal with its own personnel and office and to fill the warehouse with three months' supply of leather. Dorn said the cost would be $100,000 and he hoped to get that amount through a government loan guarantee.[45] This request was set against a record of poor performance — for the six months leading up to March 31, 1954, the tannery was showing a loss of $17,971.47 on sales of $14,728.47.

Smallwood's patience with Dorn had worn thin. Writing Pushie at the Royal York Hotel in Toronto, Smallwood detailed

42 Letter, Pushie to Horst Koch, undated. File 3.08.090. JRS Collection.
43 Letter, Smallwood to Dorn. October 13, 1953. File 3.08.098. JRS Collection
44 Letter, Dorn to Pushie, March 29, 1954. File 3.08.098. JRS Collection
45 Ibid

Finance Minister Greg Power, Joey Smallwood, and Alfred Valdmanis hold packets of medallions, after an audience with Pope Pius XII at Castel Gondolfo, 1952 (CNS Archives, Coll 075 — 5.04.745)

49

Equipment arrives at Corner Brook for construction of the cement plant, December 20, 1952 (CNS Archives, Coll 075 — 5.04.509)

United Cotton Mills, one of two textile mills established in St. John's under the industrialization program. (CNS Archives, Coll 075 — 5.03.369)

Products from Terra Nova Textiles and Newfoundland Hardwoods at an Industrial Exhibition, early 1950's. (CNS Archives, Coll 075 — 5.04.229)

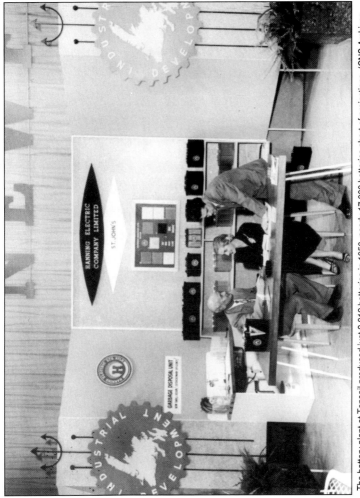

The battery plant at Topsail produced just 3,312 batteries in 1956, nearly 17,000 batteries short of projections. (CNS Archives Coll 075 — 5.04.273)

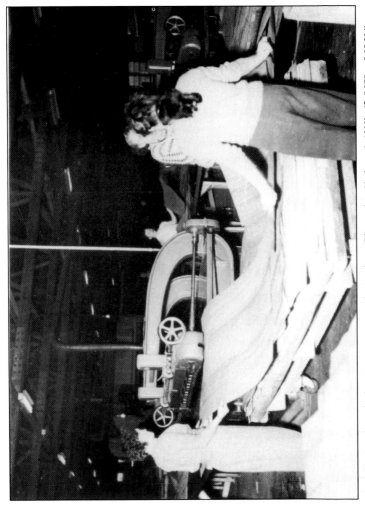

Atlantic Hardwoods survived as a government-owned enterprise until it was closed in the early 1990's. (Coll 075 — 5.05.394)

Children hold "Buy Newfoundland" posters, part of a campaign by Newfoundland manufacturers in the face of competition from Canadian manufacturers. (CNS Archives, Coll 650)

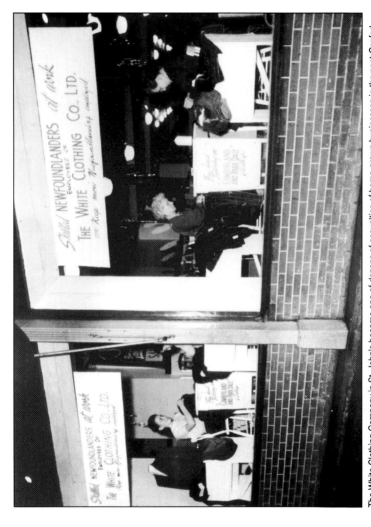

The White Clothing Company in St. John's became one of dozens of casualties of home-grown businesses in the post-Confederation period. (CNS Archives, Coll 075 — 5.04.643)

Dorn's request. He asked Pushie to investigate the possibility of renting warehouse space in Montreal and stated emphatically, "I certainly have no intention of advancing any hundred thousand dollars to him."[46]

Major orders did come into the tannery, some of which it filled and others which were filled unsatisfactorily. One of the unsatisfactory ones was a demand for hockey shoe leather from the Eagle Shoe Company Limited. The results were diastrous. It was found that in the two week interval between when Eagle cut the leather for the skate lining and the skate's assembly, "...the lining was two sizes smaller than the corresponding upper." The company claimed independent studies had shown "the leather delivered was still wet and subject to shrinkage at the time of cutting." Eagle demanded $1,282.38 from the tannery if the contract was renewed, and double that if it was not renewed.[47]

This was not the type of publicity the tannery wanted. And the problems were not confined to markets on the mainland. At home, the early good relations with Gold Sail would soon come to a crashing end. Less than nine months after its intervention to have the government protect the tannery, Gold Sail was asked by the government to respond to complaints about the handbags it produced. Gordon Pushie informed the company there were complaints the clasps were not holding, "parts coming unglued" and "handles cutting away from the bags." Wrote Pushie,

> It should be realized that prompt action should be taken by the company to settle such complaints. Nothing could damage your operations more than to have raised around St. John's that your product wasn't standing up well.[48]

Gold Sail responded to the complaints with unrestrained vigour and anger, all of it directed at the tannery, the firm it had so eagerly supported less than nine months before. Of the problem with its handbags, Gold Sail wrote, "...they stem not

46 Letter, Smallwood to Pushie, May 28, 1954. File 3.08.098. JRS Collection
47 Letter, Eagle Shoe Company Limited to Donald Dawe, lawyer for Newfoundland Tannery (Wm. Dorn) Limited, January 27, 1958. 3.08.099. JRS Collection.
48 Letter, Pushie to Gold Sail, December 16, 1954. File 3.08.084. JRS Collection

from poor workmanship but from inferior raw material from the tannery in Carbonear."[49]

Gold Sail's letter continued,

We have tried...to work in close co-operation with the tannery using their leather. The result has been loss of prestige for our product and a shift in purchasing from Carbonear to other suppliers...You have, we believe, copies of letters from our firm to the tannery, presently in your possession on this subject of inferior leathers, and belated deliveries.[50]

The balance sheets of both Gold Sail and the tannery had taken a battering. Both companies lost money in all the years they operated. By the time the tannery was closed in 1957, it had run up a deficit of well over $120,000.[51] Gold Sail's deficit had reached more than $203,000 by the time it went out of business in 1960.[52]

The Conception Bay plants, as they were referred to by Gordon Pushie,[53] were part of a government strategy to industrialize the Conception Bay North area. This strategy was made clear to the German interests behind the proposal for the shoe factory (which became Koch Shoes at Harbour Grace). Notifying the principals that government had approved a loan for the shoe factory, the Assistant Director General of Economic Development, A.L. Graudins, underlined that the approval was contingent on the factory being constructed in Carbonear, "instead of St. John's". The letter stated it was government's intention for "the Harbour Grace-Carbonear area to become a new centre of industries..."[54] The government planned to round out its program in the area with a marine oil hardening plant, a margarine and shortening plant and a soap factory.[55]

49 Letter, Gold Sail to Pushie, December 23, 1954. File 3.08.084. JRS Collection
50 Ibid
51 File 3.08.100. JRS Collection. [The final figure is not available in the records. $121,439.17 represents losses for the period to September 30, 1955.]
52 Annual Financial Statements. File 3.08.085. JRS Collection. The exact amount was $203,867.33 to December 31, 1960.
53 Memo, Pushie to Executive Council, September 11, 1957. File 2.08.008. JRS Collection.
54 Letter, A.L. Graudins to Mr. R. Rieher, Tuttlingen, Germany, February 9, 1952. File 3.08.097. JRS Collection

None of those plants made it to fruition, but a knitting mill did figure in the plans for one of Conception Bay North's longest established communities.

Eckhardt Knitting Mills was established at Brigus in 1953 on the former premises of Riverside Knitting Mills. Started with a $387,400 loan from the government, the mill was to produce fine knitwear. The plant was begun by Alfons Bernhard Eckhardt, a veteran in the Austrian knitwear business. The company's brochures boasted Italian styling and Austrian know-how, a combination that the government hoped would launch the company toward large profits.

Smallwood declared employment at the mill would reach 300 to 400 when full production was reached. At first, it appeared the Eckhardt mill was more forward-looking than the industries already established, most of which had "jumped into production without paying too much attention to market possibilities and outlets."[56] Eckhardt proposed to overcome that pitfall by establishing outlets in the central Canadian fashion centres of Montreal and Toronto. The local market would be serviced from an outlet on Water Street in St. John's. Eckhardt chose the name Irene Knitwear Limited.

A year-and-a-half after the mill went into production, Eckhardt ran short of operating capital, and asked the government for $160,000. In recommending cabinet approve the application, Pushie advised the government to attach stringent conditions to the loan and to insist on the appointment of a government director to the board. (These appointments became a pattern for most of the industries that requested and were given additional funds.) By accepting the additional assistance, Eckhardt lost some of its independence, as the government-appointed director (Gordon Pushie) had "power to control expenditures" and authority to ensure "that no salaries be paid to non-residents of Newfoundland" without his written approval.[57]

Government was not pleased with the way the mill was run, as was evident in a letter Pushie sent to a New York man the

---

55 Ibid
56 *Financial Post*, July 2, 1955, Vol. 49. p. 26.
57 Memo, Pushie to Cyril Greene, Attorney General Department. December 28, 1954. File 3.08.102. JRS Collection

government had enlisted to scout potential buyers for the mill. Calling it "one of the best individual enterprises to be set up under the Newfoundland Government's development program", Pushie said the plant was nonetheless on the market, as "we regard it [the present operators] as a purely temporary setup until such time as the plant will be taken over by an experienced company which has the organization to handle both the design and the styling of the garments as well as the sales staff to handle the output."[58]

Some of the problems with the mill were explained to the board of directors in letters from the manager of the St. John's store. While sales for 1956 had improved 100-percent over 1955 ($128,467.33 compared to $61,517.66), the store manager complained they "could have sold $10,000 more if we had not been handicapped by not having the popular wool colours."[59] The manager noted that for "two days alone in Christmas week", the store lost sales for 100 jackets at $25 each. The Montreal office was reporting similar problems.

> ...we are still having insufficient supply of a variety of best-selling articles which were ordered long ago and on several occasions.[60]

The shortage of products in the popular colours continued through the late 1950's. But why? Some of the answers were given in a 1957 analysis of Eckhardt Mills by Arthur D. Little, Inc., in its survey of the new industries for the government. The survey dealt a blow to the credo of a company dedicated to selling fashionable women's knitwear. "...Eckhardt has not kept up with styling" the report charged, noting "there has been no change in the style of the Eckhardt lines since it [sic] was first introduced in 1955."[61] The report presented an unflattering

58 Letter, Pushie to Abner Goldstone, New York. December 15, 1955. File 3.08.102. JRS Collection
59 Letter, Mary Ann Shaw to Board of Eckhardt Knitting Mills, January 6, 1957. File 3.08.102. JRS Collection
60 Letter, Irene Knitwear, Montreal to Pushie. January 23, 1956. File 3.08.102. JRS Collection
61 Draft Report to the Province of Newfoundland, "Analysis of Eckhardt Mills Limited" by Arthur D. Little, Inc. September 11, 1957. File 3.08.104. JRS Collection

image of the factory's general manager who "indicated that production for inventory is made according to what he considers will sell rather than according to lines which have proven themselves in the marketplace."[62] Sportswear buyers critiqued the company's line with unreserved bluntness, using phrases such as "too germanic...Very Teutonic...finish antiquated...old hat English".[63]

Smallwood revealed how some of Eckhardt's problems had come about, in a memo that he circulated to cabinet on the day the Little draft report was presented to the government. He explained that Eckhardt, through its retail outlet, Irene Knitwear, was also the selling agent for the shoe, handbag and glove factories. This arrangement created a problem for Eckhardt, as the company was required to use its own meagre working capital for prepayment of goods from the other factories. Smallwood indicated the strategy was a necessary one, as only in this fashion had it "been possible to meet emergencies in these other plants."[64] He acknowledged the pressure this placed on Eckhardt's working capital, causing it problems "meeting drafts for wool."[65] Smallwood urged the cabinet to increase the mill's working capital with a $40,000 loan guarantee.[66] Eckhardt continued to operate, but with financial difficulties, until it was forced to close in the early 1960's. Smallwood's memo underscored the poor financial state of the industries, and reinforced that most, if not all of them, were operating under questionable business practices.

The Conception Bay plants though, were not alone in their failure to perform well. In the St. John's area, several industries battled a sea of red ink.

THE MACHINERY PLANT

The machinery plant at Topsail was expected to put Newfoundland on the map in heavy industrial manufacturing. But the plant that was launched with so much fanfare just before the

---

62 Ibid
63 Ibid
64 Memo, Smallwood to Cabinet, September 11, 1957. File 2.08.008. JRS Collection
65 Ibid
66 Ibid

1951 general election, proved early on to be a big money loser. Unable to attract the large defense contracts contemplated in the early days, CMIC was reduced to becoming "just a fairly large machine shop".[67]

CMIC benefited from the government's decision in the fall of 1953 to postpone interest payments on guaranteed loans for all the new industries, but this clearly was not enough. Writing to Smallwood in the early spring of 1955, CMIC's vice-president, Dr. E. Roethe, disclosed financial statements so poor that he felt it was "practically impossible for our company to obtain any short-term credits from a bank."[68] Roethe complained that promised price advantages of 10-15% for Newfoundland firms competing with mainland firms for defense orders "did not materialize." This, he went on, combined with "a very limited amount of private orders", resulted both in lower levels of employment than expected and in the company's inability to earn interest and depreciation."[69]

Citing an accumulated debt of $460,380.72, Roethe told Smallwood the only solution to the company's problems was a change in the existing agreement that would relieve CMIC from paying interest on its loan until it made a profit.[70] This was as much as asking that the loans be written off, as the plant was coming to rely primarily on making spare parts for equipment in the other new industries, a few construction jobs and the occasional United States Air Force contract.

The government did not yield to Roethe's request, as doing so would unquestionably have created a precedent other industries would ask to have extended to their operations. Such a move would also have admitted failure of the program, a step Smallwood was unwilling to take in the early 1950's. This decision effectively concealed poor performance, and it did nothing to slow the momentum that was exerting overwhelming pressure on the financial statements of most of the new industries. The machinery plant would eventually be sold to the

67 Horwood, p.181
68 Letter, Dr. E. Roethe, CMIC to Smallwood, March 28, 1953. pp.5-6. File 3.08.058. JRS Collection
69 IBID
70 IBID

private sector, before closing in the 1980's. (By the early 1990's, the property had been converted to a vinyl window manufacturing plant.)

THE OTHER INDUSTRIES

After the machinery, cement and hardwoods plants, United Cotton Mills carried the largest public investment. The rhetoric surrounding the announcement of this St. John's-based plant confirmed the part fact — part fantasy approach of Smallwood toward selling his program to the public. He boasted of 800 jobs at United Cotton Mills, a figure in line with what its German principals had estimated. What Smallwood did not say publicly, but what the Germans clearly said in their private proposals before construction started, was that the plant would get started with 50 Newfoundland workers, to be increased to "250 people and more later."[71] The plant was to include spinning, weaving and fabricating mills. The impression given in public was that while the entire mill would not be up and running at once, it would be operational and the 800 jobs in place in short order. It was clear from information the Germans sent to Smallwood prior to the public announcement, that the future shape of the plant was far from finalized. The Germans made the information available to the government in order that Smallwood might answer questions in the House "and in justifying the commitment of public funds..."[72] Insofar as the weaving plant was concerned, the Germans said it seemed a little early "to give exact details about the proposed manufacturing program and this also refers to the spinning."[73]

Even with this uncertainty about the future shape and size of the plant, the Germans predicted a profit of $322,375 from the operation. They contemplated selling men's shirts and pyjamas and woman's pyjamas, aprons, and house dresses through their own sales agents in every big town in every province. Transportation costs, which would come to haunt most of the new industries, were described by the Germans as "relatively low";

---

71 Letter, Wilhelm Offen to A.L. Graudins, January 10, 1952. File 3.08.117. JRS Collection
72 Letter, Graudins to Offen, December 18, 1951. File 3.08.117. JRS Collection
73 Letter, Offen to Graudins, January 10, 1952. File 3.08.117. JRS Collection

and while they foresaw competition from both Canadian and US firms, they concluded there was "plenty of room for other textile mills in Canada."[74]

There were however, troubling signs in the North American textile industry, ones the government seemed unwilling or unable to appreciate. An Industrial Intelligence Bulletin on the textile industry from the federal Department of Trade and Commerce noted that since April 1950, "activity in the clothing industry slipped considerably."[75] A major part of the change was being brought about by the manufacture of synthetic fibres. Per capita purchases of synthetic fibre clothing had increased from 12-percent in 1939 to 21-percent just ten years later. The Trade and Commerce Department wrote that the trend to synthetic clothing "...may achieve even greater significance in the future."[76] A notation on the bulletin by Smallwood urged his then-Director of Economic Development, Alfred Valdmanis, to read part of the document that reported the "real per capita expenditure on clothing of disposable income has been below the long-term trend during the past three years."[77] Smallwood appeared to ignore the section that warned of the significant move to synthetic fibre in the clothing industry.

United Cotton Mills steadily lost money during the 1950's. By October 1961, its accumulated deficit stood at more than $569,000. During that year, the government came to the mill's rescue, and liquidated about two-thirds of the deficit, made up chiefly of operating losses and unpaid interest on the government loan. The loan itself was still outstanding. This plant too, would eventually close.

It became increasingly difficult for Smallwood to maintain that the industries were "breaking even and having their own working capital" (as he claimed in the case of money-losing Eckhardt Mills, Koch Shoes, Atlantic Gloves and Newfoundland Tanneries in 1956), when soon after those declarations, the

---

74 Ibid
75 Paper, "The Clothing and Textile Industries", Economics Division, Industrial Intelligence Division #2, Department of Trade and Commerce, Ottawa. (Undated) p.6
76 Ibid, p. 9
77 Ibid, p. 11

government would ask the legislature to approve additional guarantees for the plants. By June 1957, the government had seen enough. With about $20 million outstanding in loans to the industries and none of the accumulated $2 million in interest having been paid back to the Treasury, Smallwood announced he had enlisted the help of Arthur D. Little, Inc. of the Massachusetts Institute of Technology to assess the new industries. "The time has come to take stock" was how Smallwood explained his actions.[78] He attempted to prepare the public for the verdict, by placing the industries in various categories of financial health. Some, he said, were "in a very good healthy condition" while others "may need nothing more than an improvement of management" and still others "may prove to be discouraging".[79]

Reporting on the appointment of Arthur D. Little, Inc., the Newfoundland Journal of Commerce remarked that 1957 was a "year of decision for the new industries." The Journal appeared to have the inside track on what was happening, noting the program "will undoubtedly have to be cut back because it [the government] can no longer pump money, like blood, into the veins of industries..."[80] Strikebound Newfoundland Tanneries, the Journal wrote, was not paying its way, and the paper predicted "the strike may be the excuse the government needs at this time to wipe out the industry."[81] The era of plant construction was at an end, with even the German technical help at most of the plants having left Newfoundland.

In the early fall of 1957, Smallwood began releasing the Little findings in dribs and drabs. The reports prepared by the Little company gave detailed accounts of how the various industries were faring. But Smallwood did not release the actual accounts. Instead, he took carefully selected parts of the surveys and made those public with his own commentary. Smallwood reported that overall, the survey pointed toward a "bright future for some; others not so rosy and may need more financial aid."[82]

---

78 *Financial Post*, June 29, 1957. Vol.51, pp. 59-60
79 Ibid
80 Newfoundland Journal of Commerce. "1957 — Year of Decision for 'New Industries'". Vol.XXIV, No.8. August 1957. p.22
81 Ibid

It is instructive to differentiate between Smallwood's account of the Little survey and the survey itself. On the Hanning Electric Company battery plant on Topsail Road, the *Evening Telegram* quoted Smallwood as saying the report gave the plant "a very good reference".[83] The *Financial Post* carried a similar interpretation of Smallwood's comments.

> Economic production would be 20,000 batteries annually, which the company has not yet reached. The financial success lies in reaching this output. In the meantime, it may be necessary for the government to advance a modest amount of working capital to keep the concern going until a more permanent arrangement is made.[84]

THE LITTLE SURVEY

The Little report was more to the point: it urged that the plant be leased to a major Canadian battery manufacturer "for a minimum of five years at a rental that could be as low as $1 per year if necessary..."[85] A draft report to the government six months earlier (this predated Smallwood's announcement that the government had engaged the Little firm) was even more blunt:

> Hanning Electric Company Limited is in default in its obligation to the Newfoundland Government...Although the plant with minor equipment modifications has a productive capacity of 50,000 batteries per year, total unit sales in 1956 were only 3,312. The low sales are due to the limited replacement battery market in Newfoundland and the severe competition in that market.[86]

The draft report also said the plant was overmanned for its production level and that production below 20,000 batteries a year "is not economically justifiable".[87]

The same pattern of interpretation followed with Little's

---

82 *Financial Post*, November 30, 1957, Vol.51. p.25
83 *Evening Telegram*, November 2, 1957. p.3
84 *Financial Post*, November 30, 1957, Vol.51. p.25
85 "Conclusions", Arthur D. Little, Inc. Survey of Hanning Electric Company Limited, 1957. p.1
86 Draft Report on Hanning Electric, Arthur D. Little, Inc. March 31, 1957
87 Ibid, p.2

assessment of other industries. The *Financial Post*, relying on Smallwood's comments about North Star Cement in Corner Brook, wrote,

> Technical experts from the US who examined the plant report it is a fine enterprise with an excellent future.[88]

The Little survey was more brutal in its assessment, stating the plant "is not adequately protected by known proven deposits of limestone...the plant is too small to produce cement at costs competitive to those of larger plants...the plant is generally overmanned..." And the report made it clear the government would get only some of the financial return it expected from the industry, noting "the current level of profitability of North Star should permit at least part of the interest payments due the province."[89]

Little recommended three of the plants be closed: Newfoundland Tanneries; Gold Sail Leather Goods; and Atlantic Gloves. In addition, it recommended the hardwoods division of Newfoundland Hardwoods be closed and that Koch Shoes be closed unless the government could find a company to lease the operation. The survey recommended the two textile mills in St. John's be merged.

The survey was especially hard on the Conception Bay leather industries, calling their practices severely into question and in the process, threatening the government's goal of establishing the area as an industrial centre. "The major product of the tannery has been ungraded hockey boot leather" the Little survey reported, noting that transportation costs for raw materials and finished product represented the equivalent of a 25-40% penalty in selling price when compared to mainland tanneries.[90] The report concluded "out-of-pocket losses" for 1956 were estimated at more than $100,000, not including depreciation interest or repayment of government loans.

The story was equally gloomy on Atlantic Gloves. In 1956, gloves were sold for one-third of the manufacturing cost, the survey found. The company was "restricted to the production

---

88 *Financial Post*, November 30, 1957, p.2
89 "Conclusions", Little Survey on North Star Cement, 1957 p.1.
90 "Conclusions", Little Survey on Newfoundland Tanneries, 1957 p.1

of sport gloves", a small part of the glove market. Little reported the trend was toward fabric gloves, and that even if the company captured 100% of the sport-glove market in Canada (the report estimated the company "may supply as much as 18%..."), it would operate at only half capacity. According to Little, three factors would preclude the company from becoming profitable or merely breaking even, including the high cost of raw materials, management's weakness in both production and marketing, and "the inflexibility of an uneconomic tannery."[91]

The survey was no more kind to the glove factory's commercial neighbour, Gold Sail Leather Goods. Gold Sail produced an $8 handbag, but Little concluded that with most of the Newfoundland market dominated by the sale of imitation leather and plastic bags retailing for under $6, Gold Sail would be forced to market outside the province where it "cannot compete effectively..." An additional handicap was the lack of original designs, a major shortcoming in the "lucrative, high-fashion, exclusive-shop business." According to the survey, Gold Sail's inability to produce original designs would relegate the company to copying other designs featured in popular magazines. Forecasting continuing losses, Little recommended the plant be closed and the equipment sold.[92]

Gold Sail was managed by Erwin Koch, the operator of a second leather-based industry in Harbour Grace, Koch Shoes. The shoe factory fared slightly better than the other leather industries: the survey concluded it could operate economically if it increased production to 70,000 pairs, limited itself to 10 different styles (the company at one time featured 67 different styles), and lowered its prices. Newfoundland, the survey argued, could only take a small portion of the company's production. The company's survival therefore, would depend on substantial exports. The survey concluded however, such a strategy would impose a major challenge, as even in exporting to the low end of the Maritimes shoe market, transportation costs would make it difficult for Koch Shoes to compete with low-priced English imports. The survey recommended the

---

91 "Conclusions", Little Survey on Atlantic Gloves, 1957 p.1.
92 "Conclusions", Little Survey on Gold Sail Leather Goods, 1957 p.1

plant be leased to a new operator and that the company's wholly-owned subsidiary in Toronto — a retail outlet named Ariston Shoes Limited — be sold.[93]

The survey came down hard on the construction division of Newfoundland Hardwoods, which it claimed was losing $1000 a day, equivalent to an annual loss of $2000 for each worker. It said neither the door, plywood, nor flooring plants had any profit potential. The plywood division for example, manufactured its product from imported mahogany. Little noted the North American mills were moving away from this kind of product. That, combined with stiff competition from foreign companies having access to cheaper raw materials, would make it difficult to operate at a profit.[94] The bright spots in Newfoundland Hardwoods were two unrelated concerns — the asphalt and creosote divisions. Both divisions would later show substantial profits — the creosoting division owing much to the heavy demand for wooden poles as the electrification program gained momentum in the 1960's, and the asphalt division because of demand emanating from the paving of the Trans Canada Highway and other roads.

The Little reports concluded there was no need for two textile mills in St. John's. It called for the mills to be consolidated, with resulting "important savings" in overhead. In addition to high overhead, Little determined both Terra Nova Textiles and United Cotton Mills suffered from low productivity and small sales volume. The survey said overhead expenses at United Cotton Mills "as a percentage of direct-labour costs are approximately twice those of profitable US firms."[95]

Arthur D. Little, Inc. was not asked to comment on or evaluate the entire industrialization program, but its report amounted to a stinging rebuke for the thrust of the program. The industries that Smallwood claimed would sell to "all parts of Canada, in the United States, and in all parts of the world" were, according to the Little survey, barely able to compete in Newfoundland. Smallwood had to put on his bravest political

93 "Conclusions", Little Survey on Koch Shoes, 1957 pp.1-2.
94 "Conclusions", Little Survey on Newfoundland Hardwoods, 1957 p.1
95 "Conclusions", Little Surveys of United Cotton Mills and Terra Nova Textiles, 1957 p.1

face to proclaim in the wake of the survey that some of the industries would have a "bright" future. Some of them (North Star Cement, Atlantic Gypsum and Koch Shoes) went through various transformations and remain in business as private concerns.

Smallwood was not anxious to release the Little survey to the public. Several months after he addressed the results of the first surveys in public, a Conservative MHA, Augustine Duffy asked that the surveys be tabled in the legislature. Smallwood's reply was an emphatic no.

> Does he think sincerely that the full and intimate details of all costs and all other business secrets, contracts, prices, commissions of the North Star Cement Company should be handed over to other Cement Companies across Canada....[96]

Duffy had his own suspicions why the reports were being kept under wraps, accusing Smallwood of picking out "what he wants to make public". Duffy charged that if the reports were made public, "there would be considerable flattening out of the extravagant loans that were going on."[97] Indeed, Table 1 outlines the seriously deficient position of all the companies relative to their loan repayments.

Table 1 does not take into account the interest forgiven on loans in the first two years of the program. Neither do these figures take into account other special efforts to have interest written off by the government during this period, nor interest payments delayed until the thirteenth and fourteenth years as a result of the October 1953 decision by the government.

As Table 2 shows, by the early 1960's, most of the plants had been closed or come under new management. Newfoundland's post-Confederation experiment with government-financed manufacturing firms had come to an end. Smallwood now began to concentrate on natural resource development. Much of this attention was directed toward Labrador where huge deposits of iron ore would give rise to the towns of Labrador City and

---

96 Proceedings, January 24, 1958, p.65
97 Proceedings, January 24, 1958. p.66

Wabush. Smallwood also went in search of capital to develop Labrador's hydro potential. Around the coastline of Newfoundland and Labrador, the fishery continued to be the lifeblood that sustained hundreds of small and medium-sized communities and towns.

TABLE 1

Principal and Interest Owing on Newfoundland Government-Guaranteed Loans on March 31, 1958

COMPANY	Principal Owing on March 31, 1958	Principal/Interest Owing on March 31, 1958
A. Adler of Canada Ltd.	$ 820,000.00	$ 891,875.72
Atlantic Films and Electronics Ltd.	$ 200,000.00	$ 248,301.36
Atlantic Gloves Ltd.	$ 845,352.00	$ 967,780.97
Atlantic Gypsum Ltd.	$ 1,613,062.59	$ 1,613,062.59
Atlantic Hardboards Ltd.	$ 1,545,600.00	$ 1,830,705.79
Canadian Machinery and Industry Construction	$ 2,500,000.00	$ 3,094,013.65
Eckhardt Knitting Mills	$ 987,600.00	$ 1,103,399.7 2
Gold Sail Leather Goods	$ 220,000.00	$ 256,352.17
Hanning Electric Co. Ltd.	$ 645,000.00	$ 760,358.90
Koch Shoes Ltd.	$ 1,414,075.38	$ 1,613,401.61
Newfoundland Hardwoods	$ 4,367,217.13	$ 4,367,217.13
Newfoundland Tanneries	$ 752,208.00	$ 879,618.39
North Star Cement Ltd.	$ 4,740,000.00	$ 5,508,156.26
Superior Rubber Co. Ltd.	$ 1,600,000.00	$ 1,931,393.73
Terra Nova Textiles	$ 533,840.00	$ 595,379.62
United Cotton Mills	$ 581,699.71	$ 681,415.59
	$23,365,654.81	$26,342,433.20

SOURCE: Documents in File 3.08.064. JRS Collection.

TABLE 2

Companies Started Under Industrialization Plan and Status

COMPANY	OPENED	STATUS
A. Adler of Canada Ltd.	1956	Closed 1960
Atlantic Films and Electronics Ltd.	1953	Closed 1980's
Atlantic Gloves Ltd.	1954	Closed 1957
Atlantic Gypsum Ltd.	1952	Still in operation. Privately owned.
Atlantic Hardboards Ltd.	1952	Closed
Canadian Machinery and Industry Construction Ltd.	1952	Closed 1980's after being operated for several years by private company
Eckhardt Knitting Mills Ltd.	1955	Closed early 1960's
Gold Sail Leather Goods	1957	Closed 1960
Hanning Electric Co.	1953	Closed 1958
Koch Shoes Ltd.	1953	Still in operation as Terra Nova Shoes. Privately owned.
Newfoundland Hardwoods Ltd.	1952	Closed 1980's
Newfoundland Tanneries	1952	Closed 1957
North Star Cement Co.	1952	Still in operation. Privately owned.
Superior Rubber Co.	1953	Closed 1956
Terra Nova Textiles	1954	Sold to private interests in early 1960's. Closed 1986
United Cotton Mills	1952	Same as Terra Nova Textiles

SOURCE: Royal Commission on Employment and Unemployment (1986) Chapter 2, p.8 and JRS Collection.

CONCLUSION

In its report to the Peckford Conservative government in the mid-1980's, the Royal Commission on Employment and Unemployment likened the 1950's program to the development drive of the late 19th century, with the same disastrous results. It conceded that while the 1950's program "succeeded to a limited degree", it demonstrated "the mainland model with its urban-industrial thrust was adopted as the only desirable development mode", leaving the traditional economy "neglected."[98]

Political leaders of Smallwood's stature often get the chance to explain their actions in their memoirs. In his account of the program, Smallwood appeared struck by the criticism of his attempt at industrialization. "We put a total of about $50 million altogether in those plants..." he wrote in 1973, and while from "...a narrow, orthodox, private enterprise, balance-sheet point of view, over half of them have been losers...the fact is...they have, taken as a whole, been a profit-maker."[99] Smallwood claimed the industries put more than $50 million back into the economy in the form of wages and other disbursements, thus sparing government the cost of providing benefits to people who would otherwise have been unemployed.

Harold Horwood concluded in *Joey*, "not all the money was wasted." He pointed to the four plants that "survived after a fashion, returning nothing to the government, but giving jobs to a few hundred people."[100] Horwood referred to the program as "the Valdmanis phase of economic development". Despite his thinly-veiled disdain for Valdmanis, Horwood does credit him with proposing a moratorium on factory construction in 1952, advice which Smallwood refused.[101]

The real proof of the value of such a massive investment in secondary manufacturing is whether it changed the lot of Newfoundland's population by opening up areas of new, sustained economic activity. The Smallwood government's own economist, in a 1967 report in which Smallwood wrote the forward,

98 Royal Commission on Employment and Unemployment. Chapter 2 — "In Search of Development: An Historical Perspective". St. John's. 1985 p.7
99 Joseph R. Smallwood. I Chose Canada. Toronto:Macmillan. 1973. p.352
100Horwood, p. 183
101Horwood, p. 184

concluded not much had changed. "There can be little doubt that under-employment and unemployment have persisted with infuriating tenacity" he wrote, "despite heavy public and private investments in industry and infrastructure."[102]

The popular legacy of the industrialization drive of the late 1950's is one of failure and ineptitude. What young Newfoundlander or Labradorian has not heard with appropriate sarcasm, some variation of "that's another chocolate factory". (The current version of this line is "that's another Sprung greenhouse". Sprung was a hydroponics greenhouse financed under the Peckford Conservatives in 1987. But the time it closed in 1989, the facility had cost the Newfoundland government more than $20 million in loans and grants, plus interest.)

In the insular world of Newfoundland politics, it is often said that of all the people in the world, Newfoundlanders alone were imprudent enough to give up self-government (as they did in 1933), or that Newfoundlanders alone were gullible enough to go along with Smallwood's plan for industrialization, wasting a fortune in public funds along the way. The reality though is that there are many examples in Canada and elsewhere, of small political entities spending massive amounts of scarce public funds to try and solve the problems of underdevelopment.

102R.I. McAllister. Newfoundland and Labrador: The First Fifteen Years of Confederation. St. John's: Dicks and Company Limited, 1967. p.82

4

The Case of Nova Scotia's Industrial Estates Limited

In September 1957, the newly elected Conservative government of Nova Scotia under Premier Robert Stanfield, set out "...to encourage the promotion, expansion, diversification and development of economic activity..."[1] To achieve this goal, Stanfield established Industrial Estates Limited, a provincial crown corporation modelled on the British system of industrial estates.[2] Over the next fifteen years, IEL pursued manufacturing firms around the world with the full backing of the Nova Scotia government and the provincial treasury.

The early years of IEL's activity brought dozens of new industries to the province. Protected from political barbs by Stanfield and his government, IEL spent tens of millions of dollars luring industry to all regions of the province. IEL's first President, Frank Sobey of supermarket fame, operated with a small staff and with utmost secrecy. For 10 years, the public of Nova Scotia seemed impressed with the results of IEL's work. They returned Stanfield with a 40-6 seat majority in the 1967 general election. But soon after that, IEL's massive investments in a high-fidelity stereo manufacturing company (Clairtone) and a heavy water plant (Deuterium) started going bad. These investments resulted in a public debate about IEL (one the

---

1 Province of Nova Scotia. "Principal Agreement Between Industrial Estates Limited and the Provincial Government". September 25, 1957. p.2
2 The Nova Scotia concept involved having Industrial Estates Limited finance and build factories for industries locating to the province. The concept allowed companies to rent or enter into lease-purchase agreements. It also entailed financing equipment purchases and arranging municipal tax concessions.

political opposition revelled in) that went to the heart of the way it did business.

The incentives Nova Scotia offered business were substantial. Like Newfoundland, a high level of secrecy surrounded the Nova Scotia program. And similarly, there was little pre- or post-project assessment. Despite those similarities, the Nova Scotia program differed from Newfoundland's in a couple of key areas. IEL pursued only established companies whereas Newfoundland funded new ones. The Stanfield government left it to the board of IEL (comprised of the business elite of Nova Scotia) to court business opportunities. This placed the government in the role of banker while Stanfield accepted the "political headaches".[3]

Overall however, despite failures that cost IEL millions of dollars, Nova Scotia experienced a higher rate of success with its industries than did Newfoundland. IEL's policy of dealing with already established companies, provided at least a measure of protection for the Nova Scotia taxpayer. While tax concessions were extended to all companies and preferential rates of interest were advanced to some, the program was operated on a business-like basis and companies were required to pay back what they had borrowed. By contrast, the Newfoundland program advanced millions of dollars to enterprises that had no capital of their own. With little or none of their own resources at stake, the industrialists attracted by the Newfoundland government appeared to be poor candidates for the job of establishing and maintaining the industries that were financed. This state of affairs also cast serious doubt on the Newfoundland government's goal of recouping its investment by selling the companies to private investors. And unlike Newfoundland, Nova Scotia extracted personal guarantees from investors, a move that forced business to share some of the risk. That approach was deemed to be successful.[4]

Nova Scotia's approach to industrial development is not presented here as a point-by-point comparison to what hap-

3   James Bickerton. Nova Scotia, Ottawa and the Politics of Regional Development. (Toronto: University of Toronto Press) 1990. p. 146
4   Roy E. George. The Life and Times of Industrial Estates Limited. (Halifax: Institute of Public Affairs, Dalhousie University). Paper No.93. 1974. p.4

pened in Newfoundland. As was stated above, it is similar in some ways and different in others. The value in sketching the IEL program is that it represents an attempt to deal with under-development by a province that is similar in many ways to Newfoundland.

. . . . .

By 1957, Nova Scotia was a veteran of ninety years inside the Canadian federation. Yet, despite the suggestion nearly a century before that the Maritimes "would develop into the work-shop of the new dominion",[5] the promise was not realized. Indeed, the prevailing sentiment was that "Ontario and Quebec had been double-crossing them ever since 1867...imposing tariff, trade, transportation, political and financial policies to milk the Maritimes and crush local industry."[6] When it came to cold economic statistics, Nova Scotia lagged behind the nation. Its population was in decline relative to the nation; it was unable to close the gap on per capita personal income (Nova Scotia's was about three-quarters of the Canadian average); and new investment in Nova Scotia was only half of the national average.[7] The resulting picture was that in the 17-year period from 1940 to the inception of IEL, Nova Scotia's Gross Provincial Product increased by 76 percent, while Canada's national economy grew by 119 percent.[8]

This was the set of circumstances that lay in wait for Robert Lorne Stanfield when his Conservative party came to power in Nova Scotia in late 1956. Stanfield promised during that campaign to do something to bring the economy around. He spoke of setting up a Nova Scotia Development Corporation, although "he had no precise idea of what it would be or do..."[9] The agency that eventually got launched was Industrial Estates Limited, a

5 David Alexander. Atlantic Canada and Confederation [Essays in Canadian Political Economy]. Compiled by Eric W. Sager, Lewis R. Fischer and Stuart O. Pierson. (Toronto: University of Toronto Press). Published in association with Memorial University of Newfoundland. 1983. pp. 50-51
6 Harry Bruce. Frank Sobey: The Man and the Empire. (Toronto: Macmillan of Canada) 1985. p.242
7 Nova Scotia Voluntary Planning Board. First Plan for Economic Development to 1968. February 1966. pp.24-25
8 Bickerton, p.98
9 Bruce, p.245

crown company that was to be started with government-guaranteed loans of $12-million. It was believed IEL would eventually build a credit rating that would allow it to borrow its own funds.[10] IEL never did borrow long-term funds on its own, although its authorized borrowing limit eventually reached $200-million in 1971.[11]

There are many similarities between IEL and earlier efforts by the Smallwood government to increase industrial activity. For these and other reasons, it is instructive to look at what happened in both provinces.

In an overall way, Newfoundland and Nova Scotia interfered in their economies in a major way to try and increase the level of economic development.

The establishment of IEL in Nova Scotia was proof that responsibility for the granting of business incentives was being transferred from the municipal level of government to the provincial level. Prior to 1930, it was common for municipalities to extend help in the form of "grants, loans, bond guarantees, land gifts, and tax exemptions."[12] After the Depression, this kind of economic inducement was seen as the proper role of the provinces, as was evidenced in the growing number of provincial loan agencies dedicated to financing economic development.[13]

There were some key differences between the approach taken by IEL and that followed by Newfoundland. Perhaps the two most important differences relate to the type of industry they pursued and the involvement of political leaders in the two provinces in the running of their industrial programs.

IEL was interested in attracting established, secondary manufacturing firms, thereby staying away from financing new companies. (Even this approach however, did not prevent the loss of $70-million in the spectacular collapse of Clairtone and Deuterium.) The goal was to assist existing industries that did not compete with firms already in business, not to prop up

---

10 George, p.25
11 Ibid
12 Atlantic Provinces Economic Council. The Atlantic Economy. [Seventh Annual Review] October 1973. p.19 [This document will be referred to as APEC in later citations in this paper.]
13 Ibid, pp.19-20

"ailing industries."[14] Indeed the first chairman of IEL's board —
supermarket magnate Frank Sobey, openly said IEL "should
never accept a client with insufficient capital to run a business
and repay its debt."[15] Quite the opposite was true in Newfoundland, where Smallwood and Valdmanis appeared to be search-
ing out know-how, rather than people with deep pockets and
abundant business acumen. And although the government's
policy in Newfoundland was to lend money to the plants it
started, these became de facto grants, since only a tiny percentage of the money was ever repaid. By contrast, Nova Scotia was
more vigilant with its "loans only" policy, and it was committed
to lending money solely to companies that demonstrated an
acceptable independent capital base. But even this ironclad
policy was changeable if the potential catch was a major one.
Consequently, the "loans only" policy was altered on two occasions in the mid-1960's to allow IEL to invest directly in two big
new clients — Clairtone and Deuterium.

Frank Sobey presided over IEL's board during "...the Gold-
en Years", a time "when success followed success" and "...when
it seemed everything IEL touched was turning into glittering
new enterprises..."[16] IEL carried on its role with little government interference. "We would have no political discussions
with any members of the government, with the exception of Mr.
Manson", (a cabinet minister and the government appointee on
IEL's board of directors) Sobey said years later.[17] Just to make
sure the government understood its role, ground rules were
established early in IEL's mandate about announcements regarding new industries where the agency was involved. The
agreement was that IEL, not the government, would make all
such announcements, and then only after all the paperwork was
done.[18] This was very much different from what had happened
in Newfoundland, where Smallwood was front and centre of
every effort to land new industry. Many of the Newfoundland
industries were announced far in advance of their being estab-

14 George, p.10
15 Bruce, p.254
16 Industrial Estates Limited. Annual Report. 1982. p.4
17 Bruce, p.248
18 Ibid, p.248

lished. In the case of some industries, such as the machinery
plant at Octagon and the textile mill in St. John's, Smallwood's
public pronouncements dramatically overstated both the size of
the industries and the number of people who would find work.

. . . . .

The Nova Scotia strategy was based on a package of incentives,
including the provision of land, custom-built factories and production machinery at attractive rates of interest. A company
taking advantage of IEL assistance could receive up to 100
percent of the cost of land and buildings, either through a
lease-purchase arrangement or a loan. Firms could also get
loans for 60 percent to cover the cost of buying machinery (some
loans went as high as 80 percent.[19]) Interest was charged at the
rate the Nova Scotia government was paying, plus a small
percentage to cover the government's borrowing costs. This
was considered an attractive feature, since the Nova Scotia
government could borrow at lower rates of interest from the
banks than could private companies.[20] Some firms, automobile
tire manufacturer Michelin was an example, got a discount rate
from IEL. In Michelin's case, IEL loaned the firm $50 million for
twenty years at 3½ percent below what IEL needed to cover its
cost, a subsidy that would cost Nova Scotia $30 million over the
life of the agreement.[21] As if this was not enough to entice firms,
or perhaps as an example of what was necessary to get the job
done, municipalities were permitted to offer steep discounts in
their tax rates to businesses assisted by IEL. Many municipalities were only too eager to help out, proof that the evolution of
business incentives from local to provincial governments, was
only partway complete. Taken together, the Nova Scotia package constituted an attractive offer for business, having the effect
of spreading low capital costs over many years, thereby substantially reducing the cost of doing business.

The strategy raised an important question — if something
was good for IEL and good for business, did that necessarily
mean it was good for the Nova Scotia taxpayer? The first sub-

19 APEC, p.44
20 George, p.26
21 Ibid, p.106

stantial study of IEL was published in 1974 by Dalhousie University economist, Roy George. George found that overall, IEL had made a positive contribution to Nova Scotia.[22] He referred to the package of inducements offered by IEL as "the bait", and wrote that of the 77 plants financed through to the early 1970's, 56 (73 percent) were still in business. The 21 (27 percent) that failed however, represented 41 percent of the total investment by IEL under the program.[23] The huge loses at Clairtone and Deuterium in the late 1960's would lead to intense scrutiny of IEL, a major change from the way IEL was perceived and treated in its first decade. In those years, critics were silenced both by the apparent accomplishments at IEL and the agency's penchant for secrecy.

· · · · ·

Starting in 1960, IEL began to generate positive headlines that continued unabated for the next several years. The business press was on to the story of what was happening in Nova Scotia. IEL built six plants with eleven more underway, enough for the *Financial Post* to proclaim IEL had been transformed "...from a fledgling crown corporation to a sturdy agency for the promotion of secondary industry in Nova Scotia."[24]

The six plants IEL had already financed included an Italian knitwear firm at Pictou, a boat and furniture factory at Digby, an electronics company at Dartmouth, a ship repair business at Lunenburg, and a wood products plant at Springhill.[25] This was just the beginning however, as IEL's team literally began travelling the globe, selling both Nova Scotia and its industrial assistance program.

The chief salesman was Robert Manuge, who earned the title "Nova Scotia's globe-trotting super-salesman".[26] Manuge was reputed to have travelled two million miles on IEL business, making "as many calls as he could without collapsing..."[27]

IEL typically sent out letters to firms explaining its role and

22 Ibid, p.121
23 Ibid, p.76
24 *Financial Post*, January 2, 1960. p.2
25 Ibid, p.2
26 George, p.31
27 Bruce, p.266

the assistance it could offer. There was nothing extraordinary in that, for, as in most businesses, salesmen followed up those letters with personal calls. Four years after its inception however, IEL got some "big-time" assistance when it named an advisory board, "an international network of highly placed bluenose old boys to give the agency prestige, advice, information, and sometimes an entree."[28] These "old boys" were in some of the top positions in Canadian and US corporations. It appears they were retained as much for their high-level contacts and 'door-opening' skills as they were for business advice.

The whole formula — the financial inducements, Nova Scotia's growing credibility with business, the people IEL sent calling — all seemed to work. The early to mid-1960's was a period of breath-taking expansion, necessitating the government to expand IEL's capital base on several occasions.[29] It seemed the province's "crack sales and promotional team" was trying to drum up a new image for Nova Scotia as well as new business. "We are tired of being pictured as a province of fishermen and unemployed miners", the deputy minister of Finance and Industry said. "The only time people hear of our province is when a ship sinks or a mine closes."[30] IEL was doing its best to change that image, having concluded twenty-six agreements with firms before its fifth year in business.[31]

By 1963, IEL was going into high gear. In that year, it reached agreement with the Swedish car manufacturer Volvo, to establish an assembly plant at Dartmouth. The Volvo opening by Prince Bertil of Sweden was seen by some as more than the mere arrival of another firm. "It served as a signal to other international corporate giants," Harry Bruce wrote, "and they came to Nova Scotia thick and fast."[32] The carpet manufacturer Crossley Karastan settled in Truro, the Reynolds can factory came to Dartmouth, Canada Cement was located at Brookfield, and Deuterium was to build a heavy water plant at Glace Bay.

---

28 Ibid, p.269
29 George, p.25. [IEL's original authorized loan base was $12 million. This was increased to $18 million in 1963; $50 million in 1964; $60-million in 1966; $100-million in 1967; $150 million in 1969; $200 million in 1971.]
30 *Financial Post*, September 29, 1962. p.5
31 *Financial Post*, January 12, 1963. p.40
32 Bruce, p.277

The attraction of new industry earned accolades both for IEL and Premier Robert Stanfield. Maclean's wrote that given certain machinations with John Diefenbaker's leadership of the federal Conservative Party, "then the next leader of the federal Conservatives will likely be the bony Premier of Nova Scotia, Robert L. Stanfield."[33]

In the wake of such accomplishments, IEL appeared untouchable. The Volvo arrival at Dartmouth "had silenced all but the most partisan or axe-grinding of IEL's critics".[34] Still, those golden days of 1963 sowed the seeds for later scrutiny of the way IEL did business and it would pave the way for the departure of its first President, Frank Sobey.

. . . .

There was elation in the whole of Nova Scotia when the province emerged the winner in the 1963 sweepstakes to build a heavy water plant to meet the needs of Atomic Energy of Canada's nuclear reactors in Canada and abroad. Nova Scotia got the plant after a political battle against interests that supported a site in Western Canada, and with the help of a rising Cape Breton star in national politics, Allan MacEachen.

The heavy water plant was to be built at Glace Bay in economically-depressed Cape Breton, at a cost of $30 million, and financed with $12 million from IEL (its first venture into equity financing), an amount that represented about 40 percent of the cost. The remaining capital would be raised by Deuterium Corporation of New York. Its president, Jerome Spevack, had pioneered the concept of using salt water to produce heavy water. Salt water from the Atlantic would wind its way through miles of stainless steel piping at the new plant. Through a process that involved mixing the water with hydrogen sulphide gas, and taking the water through several hot and cold stages, heavy water would be produced.[35] That was the plan. But in reality, Deuterium was headed for trouble. The salt water technology Spevack had pioneered "corroded the pipes and other

---

33 *Maclean's*, November 16, 1963.
34 Bruce, p. 277
35 Philip Mathias. Forced Growth (Toronto: James Lewis and Samuel, Publishers) 1971. p.106

equipment, rendering the plant inoperable."[36] Spevack denied salt water was the cause of the problem, but eventually, he was ousted as president of Deuterium of Canada Limited (DCL). IEL put $15-million more into the plant, since DCL was unable to raise its share of the capital. Costs kept mounting, and by the time the plant produced its first drum of heavy water in 1976, the pricetag had climbed to $250 million. The Nova Scotia government took over IEL's investment in the plant and invested even more money of its own. That investment amounted to $135 million by the time the plant opened. In addition to that, Atomic Energy of Canada Limited (AECL) had to spend $95 million to refurbish the Glace Bay facility, in order to be spared the alternative —a $135 million pricetag for a new plant.

The Deuterium debacle demonstrated the shortcoming of the policy of maintaining a small staff at IEL and the apparent absence of expertise within the provincial civil service to assess risks such as those inherent in investing tens of millions of dollars in a heavy water plant.

There is disagreement about whether IEL had ever wanted to become involved in the heavy water project. James Bickerton claims the project was "dumped" on IEL "because the provincial government had none of the requisite negotiating or management expertise within the ranks of its own bureaucracy."[37] Roy George claims however, that while the Nova Scotia government played a prominent role in bringing the project to the province, "influential IEL directors were very active in setting up and directing the project and the IEL board was obviously eager to be involved."[38]

Management of the project was another question. How could an original $12 million Nova Scotia investment balloon to more than ten times that much? George claimed it was too simplistic to place all the blame on design faults, since $100 million had been spent by the time those flaws were discovered,[39] more than three times the original estimate of the cost. "IEL must shoulder the major responsibility" he wrote, "since

---

36 George, p.81
37 Bickerton, p.236
38 George, p.79
39 Ibid, p.84

IEL nominated its own directors to fill the majority of seats and therefore had the power to control all activities..."[40]

Unfortunately for IEL and the Nova Scotia government, Deuterium was not the only industry causing problems. Clairtone — a high fidelity stereo manufacturing company —was enticed to move from Ontario to Stellarton with nearly $8 million in the form of an IEL guarantee. The move to Nova Scotia brought 600 new jobs. "The mood everywhere was jubilation", wrote Garth Hopkins in his book on Clairtone.[41] Everywhere, it seemed, but in Ontario, where newspaper editorialists wondered if that province was beginning to lose its preeminent industrial status to Nova Scotia.[42]

Nova Scotia paid a steep price to get Clairtone. Along with the loan guarantee, IEL waived interest for three years on the loan payback. The agency also built a new plant for Clairtone and the company benefitted from a $1 million "settling-in" bonus. Federal regional development incentives were also a part of the picture, including a three-year federal tax holiday and accelerated depreciation on Clairtone's plant and buildings.[43] And there was more: Clairtone would benefit from a 30-percent freight subsidy under the Maritime Freight Rate Act; it took advantage of federal grants to train its workforce; and it received a reduced municipal tax rate for ten years.[44]

At first, the huge public investment in Clairtone appeared to pay off. The results for 1966 were good, as the company's sales "rose by more than forty percent and profits more than doubled."[45] But 1967 and subsequent years proved to be disastrous. Losses in 1967, 1968, 1969 and 1970 were $6.7 million, $9 million, $3 million, and $7 million respectively.[46]

The losses in 1967 prompted Clairtone to go back to IEL for more capital to sustain its operations. IEL, concerned both about the losses and with Clairtone's move into the colour television

---

40 Ibid, p.84
41 Hopkins, Garth. Clairtone [The Rise and Fall of a Business Empire] (Toronto: McClelland and Stewart) 1978. p.90
42 Ibid, p.90
43 Hopkins, p.92
44 Ibid, p.92
45 George, p.86
46 Ibid, p.86 and Bickerton, p.236

business, set a stringent condition — the $2 million Clairtone requested would only be granted if the company's owners surrendered control. For Clairtone, it was either that arrangement or bankruptcy. In August 1967, control of the company was handed over to IEL. Harry Bruce concluded "IEL had bought a bummer".[47] Clairtone was closed in 1972. By that time, the Nova Scotia government had bought the company from IEL and along with it, $26 million in debt.[48]

The problems with Clairtone brought about a period of intense scrutiny of IEL and its way of doing business. There was the question of whether IEL forced Clairtone into manufacturing colour television sets. Or was it the provincial cabinet that forced Clairtone into the colour television manufacturing business, in order to get the company to abandon plans to build an assembly plant for Japanese automobiles at the former Point Edward naval base on Cape Breton Island? Whoever promoted the scheme, the decision to manufacture colour televisions was a disaster. And it affected more than Clairtone. The move to colour television broadcasts in late 1965 did not result in the expected massive buying of colour sets. Having "bought heavily in the fall, building up inventory to supply a surging demand that didn't develop," dealers stopped placing more orders.[49] Clairtone ended 1966 with more than $3 million worth of colour sets that nobody seemed to want.[50]

The "ill-advised and overly ambitious decision"[51] to go into colour television manufacturing, came just as the North American industry was losing sales to the emerging companies of Japan.[52] Frank Sobey's IEL, which was in position to stop the bleeding at Clairtone when it took control in August 1967, did not apply the tourniquet. Sobey later said IEL did not act "because the cabinet wouldn't let me pull the rug on them."[53]

Whatever the reasons for the failure at Clairtone, and the huge cost overruns at the heavy water plant, the episodes

47 Bruce, p.299
48 Bickerton, p.235
49 Hopkins, p.118
50 Ibid, p.118
51 Bickerton, p.235
52 Bruce, p.299
53 Ibid, p.299

focused attention on IEL's method of operation. It was becoming more fashionable to criticize IEL. These criticisms seemed to carry extra weight now that the agency had invested in a couple of heavy-duty failures.

It was Frank Sobey's job to defend IEL in the face of the gathering storm. Speaking to a hearing of the Industry Committee of the legislature in March and April of 1969, Sobey held firm that despite the "recent troubles" at Clairtone, there was no reason for IEL to change the way it did business.[54] But the political landscape had changed in Nova Scotia with Robert Stanfield's move to Ottawa to take on the federal Conservative leadership. In Nova Scotia, the Liberals under Gerald Regan were on the way to deposing the Conservatives. Sobey himself would leave IEL that fall.

LACK OF AN INDUSTRIAL STRATEGY

One of the main criticisms levelled at IEL was that it lacked an industrialization strategy. The Atlantic Provinces Economic Council (APEC) claimed this policy void allowed IEL to focus on attracting big outside firms to the detriment of local industry.[55] Although IEL was empowered to promote secondary industry, APEC claimed "no one has ever refined the early guidelines to an industrial strategy". APEC felt that weakness resulted in a failure to assess the kind of industry "which could make the most beneficial contribution to the province's overall development."[56] In the absence of such a strategy, "the ideas of successive managers, ministers and boards of directors could determine its direction."[57] IEL's objectives were variously expressed in terms of increasing employment or creating jobs at minimum cost, and "only occasionally, have more thoughtful and sophisticated objectives been stated."[58]

Critics claim this weakness brought about an "ad hoc, promotion-oriented approach" to attracting business to Nova Scotia.[59] They point to press reports of chance meetings with

54 *Financial Post*, June 21, 1969. p.M3
55 APEC, p.44
56 Ibid, p.45
57 Bickerton, p.237
58 George, p.8
59 Bickerton, p.237

industrialists that led to plants being established in the province. Much was made of one such meeting aboard an airplane in December 1967 between IEL general manager Robert Manuge and the wife of a French automobile manufacturing executive. The meeting eventually led to a contact with the tire maker Michelin, and the establishment of two plants in Nova Scotia.[60] (Michelin has since added a third plant.) Another story was told of a chance meeting on a Japan Airlines flight from Tokyo to Hong Kong, where Manuge was said to have "charmed Indian industrialist Govind Jolly into establishing...a $30-million hardboard manufacturing plant..."[61] APEC was unimpressed by these 'chance' meetings and concluded, "the legends of chance meetings on airplanes...are fascinating, but they do not indicate a rational approach to industrialization."[62]

Similar criticism could have been aimed at Smallwood's industrialization strategy. While there were no stories about chance meetings with wealthy industrialists in airplanes, there was near total reliance on the contacts Alfred Valdmanis made in Europe. This precluded any kind of systematic identification of industry that would be suitable for Newfoundland. Such an approach, in combination with the lack of follow-up on the various industries, was a recipe for the disaster that it became.

Both the Newfoundland program and IEL in Nova Scotia operated with a small bureaucratic staff. George wrote that this was "attributable to a deliberate policy" in the early days at IEL. The agency was of the view that "technical personnel...will be engaged as necessary." By 1968, the corporation's staff consisted of twelve people, "of whom about half were secretaries."[63] There was a feeling though, that IEL did not utilize enough outside technical help to work through the details of the various projects it was financing. APEC complained the lack of staff "limited IEL's ability to perform detailed evaluations of the proposals it receives" and that this impaired its ability to follow

---

60 David E. Osborn. "Michelin Tires Manufacturing Co. of Canada Ltd." in Mark C. Baetz and Donald H. Thain. Canadian Cases in Business-Government Relations. (Toronto: Methuen) 1985. p.131
61 Bruce, p.266
62 APEC, p.46
63 George, p.21

up applications it accepted.[64] These weaknesses, according to APEC, put "a great deal of responsibility on the board of IEL to use its business acumen to supplement staff analysis."[65] In the case of the heavy water plant at Glace Bay and concerns about whether the technology would work, IEL especially, was considered to be in over its head, given that "...few people understood the process..."[66] Even when expertise was available, IEL appeared reluctant to utilize it since "departments of the Nova Scotia civil service and other government agencies which did have some capability were never brought on side because of personality clashes."[67]

The small staff allowed IEL to carry out its business with great secrecy, at least until the agency was ready to trumpet the next new industry for Nova Scotia. The chief reason for the insistence on secrecy was Frank Sobey, who "believed only fools babbled about a deal till it was in the bag."[68] But the penchant for secrecy could exact a dear price in an agency whose enabling legislation allowed directors and provincial politicians an interest in companies IEL did business with, so long as the directors abstained from taking an active part in those discussions. In the late 1960's, there were rumours IEL directors used agency funds for their own benefit.[69] Coming at the time of the Clairtone and Deuterium fiascos, the rumours served to undermine public confidence in IEL at a time when the agency dearly needed public empathy. Having tight-lipped businessmen in charge might have seemed a good idea in the early 1960's when there was lots of praise for IEL, but it seemed to be at odds later that decade when the need arose for IEL to explain its investments in Clairtone and Deuterium. This difficulty was demonstrated in Frank Sobey's answer to a question about Clairtone in 1967. "...I'm not interested in talking to any reporters who are trying to deter and hurt development in Nova Scotia", he said, "we can let the Toronto people do that."[70]

64 APEC, p.46
65 Ibid, p.46
66 Mathias, p.118
67 George, p.32
68 Bruce, p.288
69 Ibid, p.286
70 Ibid, p.288

Frank Sobey left IEL in September 1969. To confront the gathering storm about IEL, and no doubt to try and remove the agency as an issue in the coming election, Premier G.I. Smith appointed television station owner Finlay MacDonald to the top job at IEL. The *Financial Post* reported "Finlay MacDonald's appointment has been seen as a victory for the agency's critics..."[71]

MacDonald seemed to be saying the right things. He acknowledged IEL could do with a more systematic approach to development — including conducting studies "on the types of industries that Nova Scotia could sustain". And MacDonald lamented that "because of the absence of research resources, IEL has been obliged to use a shot-gun approach."[72] It might have been enough of a confession to allow IEL to survive when the Liberals took over the government in October 1970. Under the Liberals, IEL's mandate was even to include "all industrial attraction activities in the province."[73] This enhanced role included small business loans in the province, an area both APEC[74] and George[75] considered to be serious oversights under IEL's original mandate.

IEL's last big projects were the Michelin tire plants at Bridgewater and Granton. The plants did not come cheap as IEL provided a $50 million low-interest loan[76] and later, a $14.3 million loan at the "current" rate. The Nova Scotia government granted money for capital works and assistance for worker training. In addition, municipalities provided land and slashed their tax rates. The federal government assisted too, with $16-million in regional development grants, tariff concessions on Michelin tires imported into Canada from aboard for three years and "quick write-offs were allowed on capital investment."

71 *Financial Post*, May 2, 1970. p.A-6
72 Ibid, p. A-6
73 *Financial Post*, June 19, 1971. p.38
74 APEC, p.46
75 George, pp.46-47
76 Ibid, p.92. [Michelin borrowed $50 million from IEL at an interest rate of 6 percent at a time when the Nova Scotia government was borrowing at 8.6 percent. The subsidy was even sweeter than that since IEL didn't charge its customary 1 percent for expenses. George quoted from Michelin documents claiming IEL "felt committed" to the loan in 1968 when the average borrowing rate for the Nova Scotia government was 6.05 percent.]

George suggested that about two-thirds of the $150-million cost for the two plants would be public money.[77] During the late 1980's, Michelin expanded to three plants in Nova Scotia, again with help from provincial taxpayers. The new plant at Waterville was assisted with nearly $50-million in provincial money. Michelin expected to have 4,000 employees in the province by the time that plant went into production.[78]

. . . .

By the 1980's, IEL had become a provincial development agency more concerned with meeting the funding requirements of homegrown business than with landing large industry. And supporting homegrown business meant funding people who were short of capital, the designation of a lender of last resort Stanfield and the originators of IEL were determined to avoid. IEL's 1981 annual report underlined this new role, concluding "the financing provided to clients is often in excess of the amounts which could be available through commercial sources."[79] IEL, still however, kept a vigilant eye for new business "through various sophisticated 'industrial intelligence techniques'".[80] In the depths of the 1983 recession, no one was beating a path to IEL's door. The agency funded just 14 projects for a little over $7 million. There seemed to be little glamour that year as its efforts were mostly directed to "helping...companies stay in business, thus maintaining existing jobs."[81]

IEL loaned $250 million to businesses in its first 25 years. The agency claimed the money went to companies employing more than 11,000 people. According to IEL in the early 1980's, life had become quieter than in the early days, as it "...drifted off the front pages of the newspapers, no longer a powerful magnet for accolades or a prime target for brickbats."[82]

Several of the similarities between IEL's style of operation and the Newfoundland program have been dealt with above. The obsession with secrecy and the unwillingness in both prov-

77 Ibid, pp.91-92
78 *Winnipeg Free Press*, August 4, 1988. p.8
79 Industrial Estates Limited, Annual Report, March 31, 1981. p.13
80 Ibid, p.13
81 IEL Annual Report, March 31, 1983. pp.4-5
82 IEL Annual Report, March 31, 1982. pp.4-5

inces to carry out detailed assessments on projects, are obvious ones. Similarly, both IEL and the Newfoundland government were unwilling to do any kind of systematic follow-up of industries they had sponsored. This approach raises serious questions when scarce public funds are used to finance projects that are often high-risk.

The industrial development thrust in both Nova Scotia and Newfoundland suffered from vague statements of the mission to be accomplished. The principal weakness in the case of Nova Scotia is that it left unresolved the question of responsibility for the promotion of local business. IEL funded some local businesses, but the assistance was weighted heavily in favour of outside firms by a two-to-one margin.[83] In Newfoundland, the objectives did not even seem to be as well defined as they were in Nova Scotia. Newfoundland "must develop or perish" was as detailed as the message became. The result was that a politician and his mysterious sidekick determined what industries they would attract, and then, using the surplus built during the Commission of Government period, they doled out the money to cashless industrialists, who presumably, had been players in pre-war Europe, principally Germany.

The preoccupation in Newfoundland and Nova Scotia with big industry and foreign ownership may have emanated from a belief that the long tradition of exploiting the resource sector made for a poor supply of entrepreneurship and managerial talent.[84] This factor is also assumed to have been an obstacle in the development of a Newfoundland business culture capable of taking charge of fisheries development in the first two decades of the twentieth century. Of that failure, David Alexander wrote, "the answer must surely rest in the weakness in entrepreneurship and capital supply."[85]

A question that must be put in assessing both development strategies, is the relative impact they had in their respective

---

83 George, p.75. [Up to 1971, out of a total investment of $158.6, IEL had invested $50.5 million (32%) in Nova Scotia-owned plants; $37 million (23%) in other Canadian-owned plants; $22.8 million (14%) in American-owned firms; and $48.3 million (30%) in other foreign-owned companies.]
84 Ibid, p.5
85 Alexander, p.15

provinces. George determined that "...on ordinary business criteria IEL has proved a fiasco,..." But he argued, the assessment of such a program must extend past the bottom line. He judged "the province's material standard of life is higher for IEL having been born", although "there is...no indication IEL has succeeded in reducing Nova Scotia's lag in the development of its manufacturing sector."[86]

An APEC study in 1987 noted "only a slight narrowing of the gap" in manufacturing between Atlantic Canada and the national average since 1959.[87] In Nova Scotia, there has been an improvement in value-added exports. These improvements accounted for 11 percent of all exports in 1986, a strong improvement over 3 percent in 1970. Tire production at the Michelin plants represented a large part of the increase.[88] For Nova Scotia as a whole then, did the $250 million advanced to firms by IEL (to 1982), help transform it from the "province of fishermen and unemployed miners" to a modern and competitive manufacturing centre? APEC's opinion was that while "there is a little more diversity in Nova Scotia's manufacturing, fish processing and pulp and paper products still dominate."[89]

Another pertinent question centres on whether Newfoundland and Nova Scotia's development priorities were the right ones. Did the development dollars chase after the right industries to bring both employment and economic growth? In Newfoundland's case, with the exception of industries that had ties to local resources and a ready local market (eg. cement and gypsum mills), the answer is an unqualified no. In the case of Nova Scotia, the answer is not quite as simple. Certainly, the major losses in Clairtone and Deuterium raised important concerns about whether IEL used all the influence it had, in order to resolve the problems in both firms. Outside those losses however, IEL had many successes. Its philosophy of dealing with established firms removed many of the uncertainties and risks

---

86 George, p.122
87 Atlantic Provinces Economic Council. Atlantic Canada Today. (Halifax: Formac Publishing Limited) 1987. p.102
88 APEC, Atlantic Canada Today. p.180. [This statistic may illustrate to some extent George's reasoning that the bottom line cannot be taken as the only indicator of the success or failure of public investment in a given firm.]
89 Ibid pp.100-101

that would be present if IEL was primarily concerned with financing new companies. Established firms have reputations to protect, both with their customers and their shareholders. Newfoundland unfortunately, made little effort to link its industrial program with established firms. The preoccupation with going after German industrial expertise with no experience in the North American marketplace (a market Newfoundland would increasingly do business with after Confederation) gave all the industries a poor start. This, combined with a loan guarantee program that gave the government a de facto majority equity position without control of the company, allowed the various owners to plot their own losing strategies.

Of course, no one can guarantee the success of a business venture, whether publicly or privately funded. The best that can be done is to assess the risk that is about to be taken. Clearly, in the case of IEL, there were many deficiencies in this respect. The insistence on a small staff, while admirable as a goal, probably did the agency much harm, as the APEC report suggested. Sobey and others with IEL believed the agency's autonomy from government and bureaucratic influence would comfort the private sector. Taken too far however, such autonomy can create an air of invincibility in an organization, as it appeared to do at IEL. This situation, combined with a government only too willing to protect the agency from public and political protest, denied IEL the empathy it needed when some of its investments went bad.

IEL served a substantial public policy purpose in Nova Scotia. Private investors were not willing to come to the province in sufficient numbers under ordinary circumstances. Like Newfoundland a few years before, Nova Scotia attempted to create more favourable conditions. Could the money have been better spent doing other things? Even economists lack a crystal ball. "It is possible that, if the money had gone instead into tourism development, public works, education, health services and the like, the results would have been better still", Roy George wrote, but he confessed, "...this we do not know."[90]

For people who disapprove of using public money to pro-

---

[90] George, p.121

mote economic development, what is the answer for small economies at the margins of large trading provinces? Is it to let the areas die a slow, or maybe a rapid, economic death? Is it to deliberately depopulate economically moribund areas in the hope that people will move to larger centres (the growth centre concept that was practiced in the Newfoundland resettlement program under the Smallwood government)? Or are there other solutions to the puzzle of economic development, with a mix of government intervention, greater use of the resource base, and an emphasis on training to take advantage of the information technology era? In the late 1990's Newfoundland finds itself at another crossroads of economic development, with its rural areas rapidly losing population, and with its government pursuing a combination of the old and new economies.

In those circumstances, underdeveloped provinces such as Newfoundland and Nova Scotia will continue to try and spur economic development. For a few years, it will be a program like the one IEL offered. A new government will come along and try a different approach. Governments will keep trying because trying fosters hope, and hope often decides elections.

Societies and political units at the margins of major centres of economic development are constantly trying to conquer the barriers to development posed by long transportation distances and small population. Unfortunately, Newfoundland's record in attempting to shake off those problems has not been a good one.

5

Smallwood and Beyond

Newfoundland's first three industries were intended to be sold to the private sector. The proceeds from the sales would finance new industries, and so on, ad infinitum. But while this appeared to be a reasonable goal, it masked a major problem that would come to haunt all the new industries — who would want to buy them?

The basic problem stemmed from the lack of planning for the industrialization plan. The gypsum plant, for example, was constructed according to European production and market requirements. The plant was much smaller than the standard size of a similar American plant, and therefore could not produce enough wallboard at a low enough price to compete in that market. Ultimately, this problem appeared to be the main obstacle in selling the plant to the National Gypsum Company of Buffalo, New York. This was yet another example of poor planning, since, of what use were European design standards and production requirements for a mill whose main markets were in Newfoundland, eastern Canada (including Quebec and Ontario), and the eastern seaboard of the United States?

Similarly, poor planning added to the capital costs of another of the industries, Atlantic Hardboards. For instance, failure to anticipate the high moisture content of the Newfoundland birch to be used in the operation, prompted the company to go back to the government for additional funds to set up wood dryers on the premises. This contributed to increased costs and added to the high cost of production. One of the industries that came later — the machinery plant at Octagon — also fell victim to lack of planning, or perhaps, the mistaken value of a wink and a nod from some federal politician. At any rate, management at the plant, and indeed, the government itself, believed CMIC would benefit from national defense orders. When these orders did not materialize, the plant became in Horwood's words, "just a fairly large machine shop."[1]

Other plants encountered a litany of problems, from their inability to understand market forces (as was the case with Eckhardt Knitting Mills, the chocolate factory, the glove factory, and the battery plant) to poor quality (the rubber plant had the dubious distinction of being the leader in this category). No matter what specific problems the firms faced, the failures all stemmed from the lack of a sound business plan, if there was a plan at all.

In addition to the failure to plan, the industrialization program was hampered by Smallwood's bias toward the standard North American development model, where resources are brought to a central location and manufactured into a saleable product. The Royal Commission on Employment and Unemployment cited this as "the mainland model with its urban-industrial thrust."[2] There was a mistaken belief, the Commission argued, that location and other comparative advantage factors could somehow be overcome or defeated in the competitive marketplace. Such a bias meant scarce financial resources were wasted on export-oriented industries with little chance of survival, while an indigenous industry — the fishery — was largely ignored. This state of affairs was summarized by the-then Conservative Premier, Brian Peckford, in 1983.

> There was no mention whatsoever of the fishery. One industry piled up on top of another was somehow to bring prosperity. The fishery survived in spite of us, not because of us.[3]

Not only were opportunities, such as fisheries development, lost in the quest to industrialize. Smallwood and his government continued down the road to industrialization, apparently oblivious to the new reality under federalism. Tariff

1   Horwood, p.181
2   Royal Commission Report, Chapter 2, p.46
3   Brian A. Peckford. The Past in the Present [A Personal Perspective on Newfoundland's Future] (St. John's: Harry Cuff Publications Limited) 1983 p.55

walls that had previously protected Newfoundland's manufacturing sector and its 4,000 jobs were removed at the instant of
Confederation, thereby dramatically harming the competitive
position of most Newfoundland industries. Indeed, it caused
many to fail. In such an environment, it was foolhardy to finance
economic development to compete with already established
mainland firms without a proper market assessment.

Federalism also meant freight subsidies that made it
cheaper to transport goods. This state of affairs, combined with
the removal of tariffs, allowed mainland firms to reduce the cost
of exporting to the Newfoundland market. Newfoundland
firms could only benefit with goods where they had a locational
or competitive advantage.

Smallwood and Valdmanis could not be accused of pro-
ceeding cautiously. They personally invited industrialists to
come to Newfoundland and made deals on the basis of hand-
shakes, rather than rigorous research and analysis. Their high
personal regard for a business idea and their liking of an industrialist, were enough to open the public purse. Sadly, even when
such businesses lost large amounts of money, Smallwood's
political investment in the program deterred him from admit-
ting the mistakes. The tendency in such circumstances is for
politicians to "brazen it out" and continue to feed poorly per-
forming industries with even more taxpayers' cash. This is what
happened under Smallwood's program, and the result was that
business failures built up, one on top of the other.

Under the program, all that was required to get access to
government money was a business concept and plant machinery. Even in cases where industrialists lacked the required
machinery to constitute their equity in a given project, the
government was prepared to recognize "know-how" as meeting the equity requirements. Once the plant went into operation,
the government appeared to lack either the expertise or the
incentive — perhaps both— to oversee operations that would
eventually consume $26 million in direct loans and grants, plus
millions more in unpaid interest, without returning more than a
few token payments to the treasury. It is little wonder in those
circumstances, that most of the industries failed. As a result of
those failures, Newfoundland lost out on several counts — the
loss of the major part of its pre-Confederation cash surplus; the

lost time pursuing industry while virtually losing sight of its most important renewable industry, the fishery; and the serious lack of attention toward assisting an indigenous crop of entrepreneurs.

Finally, despite the pretension that it was private enterprise that operated under Smallwood's program, it was public money that kept the program in operation. Despite this, the government had no oversight role in the industries. It was only after repeated trips back to the government for extra operating capital, that officials demanded the new industries allow government officials on the board of directors. This state of affairs could only be described as negligence on the government's part. Sadly, it came to typify the government's approach to the industries.

NEWFOUNDLAND AND DEVELOPMENT: THE BIG PICTURE

Newfoundland is not alone in terms of the problems it has encountered in search of economic development. There are examples from around the world, extending from Canada itself to sub-Saharan Africa to Finland. A study on Finland for example, shows the two northernmost provinces were the poorest and were the most reliant on primary sector industries; they had the lowest birthrate, and their level of unemployment grew most rapidly.[4] The northern-most provinces also had the highest emigration rates.

There has also been a great deal of work done in the Caribbean, where major changes in policies and institutions, along with a move toward regional institutions have been suggested as ways to help reduce the region's level of economic dependence.[5] Similarly, the impoverished states of sub-Saharan Africa have been urged to co-operate more on a regional basis to foster economic development; the elite have been advised to give up

---

4   Britta Koshiaho. "Regional Development, the Case of Finland", pp.348-354, in Anton Kuklinski, Olli Kultalahti and Britta Koshiaho (eds.) Regional Dynamics and Socioeconomic Change (Tempere, Finland: Finnpublishers) 1979

5   William G. Demas. "Economic Independence: Conceptual and Policy Issues in the Commonwealth Caribbean", pp. 202-204, in Percy Selwyn (ed.) Development Policy in Small Countries (London: Croom Helm Ltd.) 1975

their profligate lifestyles and spend more of their money at home; national leaders have been told to abandon their national airlines and national fertilizer plants and "learn to make do with regional airlines and regional fertilizer plants."[6]

The problems of underdevelopment and uneven development have been the subject of much intense study. Two main theoretical frameworks have emerged to explain development issues — a dependency perspective, which examines the relationships of various aspects of production, including class, the role of elites, capital accumulation, and exploitation; and the orthodox economic or market analysis approach, which views the market as a self-regulating mechanism, to which all other aspects of the economic system must adhere.

Looked at through orthodox economic eyes, Newfoundland would certainly have been seen to be lacking many of the ingredients to make manufacturing industries prosper. The province is a long way from major markets and it is sparsely populated. It is a resource-dependent economy, showing some of the signs of evolving to a more developed one. The dependency perspective, on the other hand, defines the development problem as a relational one. Who controls development in a region? Is the driving force imported capital, or local capital? Are profits kept in the local economy or exported? Out of this approach has developed the concept of dependency theory, which accuses capital of being both centralist and exploitive. Some of the major works on Newfoundland political economy have been from a dependency point of view.

Summers (1993), Antler (1979), Alexander (1973) and Matthews (1983) have studied the Newfoundland problem through the critical lens of dependency theory. The term 'critical lens' is used because dependency theory implies a "turning upside down" of economic analysis, in an effort to understand the underlying factors that affect economic development. This approach differs from orthodox economic theory, such as that advanced by Courchene. He argues regional disparities are worsened by government interference (transfers, unemploy-

6 Robert S. Browne. "Africa: Time for a New Development Strategy", pp.407-408, in Michael T. Martin and Terry R. Kandal, Studies of Development and Change in the Modern World (New York: Oxford University Press) 1989

ment insurance, minimum wage laws). Courchene sees the entrenchment of regional disparities under this scenario "where provinces and regions alike are made more dependent on the system of transfers."[7] Courchene believes the market, left to its own devices, can equalize economic growth and benefits. Brewis, similarly, placed great faith in the market. Although he recognized the problems of low- or slow-growth areas, he recommended national government policies as solutions, rather than changes to the structure of the economic system itself.[8] Such an approach however, may not take into account all the factors that contribute to underdevelopment, and as a consequence, this can lead to sweeping generalizations about the reasons for underdevelopment, and therefore, result in the wrong solutions being applied.

Many of the dependency theorists who have written about Newfoundland have a deep understanding of its history of economic development. Summers traces the roots of underdevelopment to the early part of the nineteenth century. She argues local development was stymied for several reasons — the absence of capital for investment; a weak investment banking sector which impeded economic diversification; and the existence of the colonial state which "was strongly representative of English mercantile interests", and thereby opposed to diversification of Newfoundland's economy away from the fishery.[9] Summers further claims that during efforts to diversify the economy after the turn of the twentieth century, mining interests exploited the local dependence on the industry, and exacted substantial concessions, with serious implications for policy modification and change of governments.[10]

Alexander added greatly to this line of inquiry. However, rather than opting for the classic dependency approach and its

7 Courchene, Thomas J. "Analytical perspectives on the Canadian economic union", in Trebilcock, M.J., et al. Federalism and the Canadian Economic Union. (Toronto: University of Toronto Press) 1983. p.93
8 T.N. Brewis. Regional Economic Policies in Canada (Toronto: Macmillan) 1969 p.242
9 Valerie Summers. Regime Change in a Resource Economy: The Politics of Underdevelopment in Newfoundland (1825-1993) Manuscript. (St. John's) 1993 p.40
10 Summers, pp.61-71

bias against so-called 'exploitive' outside interests, Alexander focussed on the local merchants in the early twentieth century. He lamented the lack of attention given to fisheries development, which he believed "might have floated the country over its railway, war and other development-debt burdens, and introduced a dynamic into the well-being, self-confidence and initiative of the country."[11] Alexander pointed to the "inability or unwillingness of its leaders to mobilize the country to manoeuvre more effectively."[12] He argued that Confederation, instead of providing new impetus for Newfoundland economic development, confined the province to the traditional role of a peripheral province.[13]

Doug House argued effectively that Newfoundland has been hampered in the post-Confederation period by large, outside interests, beginning in the central Canadian boardrooms of the major mining and pulp and paper companies, extending to the Canadian banks and Wall Street financiers, and into the key federal government departments of Fisheries and Oceans and Mines and Energy.[14] House appeared to adopt Alexander's argument that Newfoundland's dependence is at least partially the result "of its own mistakes in the past";[15] the rest he attributes to "the centralist logic of the international expansion of a market economy..."[16]

The story of Newfoundland underdevelopment is a complex one, woven into the fabric of its time as colony, country, and now, province of Canada. It is a story rife with exploitation, from its early days as a fishing station for English merchants, to its present status as exporter of minerals, paper, and fish, and as a half-million plus captive market for Canadian consumer goods.

Dependency theory is a good starting point for the study of

11 David Alexander. "Development and Dependence in Newfoundland 1880-1970", in Acadiensis. Vol.4, No.1. Autumn 1974. p. 13
12 Ibid, p.6
13 Ibid, p.24
14 Doug House. "The Mouse that Roars: New Directions in Canadian Political Economy", p.177, in Brym, Robert J. (ed.) Regionalism in Canada (Toronto: Irwin Publishing Inc.) 1986
15 Ibid, pp. 177
16 Ibid, p.178

the Newfoundland economy, as it dares look beyond the traditional quantifiable economic indicators such as gross domestic product, income level, and the distribution of industry, to factors such as the ownership of capital. The market approach to analyzing economic underdevelopment also plays a key role, as it quantifies key aspects of economic development, thereby allowing comparisons with other areas and regions.

But theoretical approaches fail to take account of the impact of the political environment. This is an especially important point in discussing the industrialization program that Smallwood undertook in the early 1950's. Smallwood developed a program without well-articulated goals. There was no transparency to the process as far as public oversight was concerned. Industries were negotiated, deals signed, and practically open-ended finances committed. The personalities of leaders and their way of doing business are important factors in determining the shape, and likely the outcome, of government-sponsored economic development initiatives. A leader's biases and weaknesses are also likely to be reflected in how the industries perform.

POLITICS AND DEVELOPMENT PLANS

Smallwood's industrialization program is one of five distinct development stages in the post-Confederation era. The second of those five stages also happened during Smallwood's 23 years in office. That attempt at economic development lasted from the late 1950's to Smallwood's departure from power in 1972. This time, the initiative centred on megaprojects — both in the natural resource field and in large-scale industrial development.

The iron ore mines at Labrador City [1962) and Wabush [1964] were major resource developments, as was the Churchill Falls power development [late 1960's]. The mines became large employers, necessitating the construction of two large towns in the western Labrador frontier. The Churchill Falls development became the largest construction project in Newfoundland to that time, providing employment for thousands of people. There were two other major power developments during Smallwood's tenure, the Bay d'Espoir hydro project [1967] and the construction of a gas-fired electricity generating station at Holy-rood [1970].

Development of the mines in Labrador required massive amounts of capital, as did the Churchill Falls power project. Capital for the mines was provided by the big steel producers, who were anxious to obtain ore for their furnaces in central Canada and the northeastern United States. Financing for Churchill Falls came from an international consortium, and was secured in 1969 by a long-term, low-rate contract with Hydro Quebec. Newfoundland benefitted by getting most of the construction jobs, but it is Quebec that continues to enjoy the substantial financial benefits of the contract, estimated by Brian Peckford in 1983 at $2 billion since the power was turned on in 1976 [17] and by Brian Tobin at $12-$13 billion in 1997.[18] Similarly, with the mines, Newfoundland benefited from the mining jobs, but the mining companies paid little in taxes — $16.63 million from 1970 to 1975. Only with new legislation in 1975, did royalties increase to about $12 million a year.[19] (Quebec also benefits from the mines at Wabush and Labrador City — Wabush ore is pelletized at Point Noire near Sept Isles, and all the Labrador ore is taken by railway to Sept Isles for shipment to the steel mills.)

The major industrial enterprises that began under this chapter of economic development were induced by substantial subsidies. Federal subsidies on shipbuilding, and subsequent Newfoundland contributions to cover annual deficits, allowed the Marystown Shipyard [1966] to get started. The attractive point for Smallwood was the 50-percent federal subsidy for Canadian-built, steel-hulled fishing vessels over 33 metres.[20]

17 Peckford, p. 58
18 In March, 1998, Newfoundland and Quebec agreed to general principles on Lower Churchill development, and further development of the Upper Churchill. Part of that deal included extra revenue for making available to Quebec a guaranteed supply of power during the winter. Quebec also waived the three-year recall notice on 130 MW of power available to Newfoundland, and allowed the province to immediately sell that power at current market rates back into the Quebec power grid. The two provinces agreed to conclude a legal agreement by December 15, 1998.
19 Peckford, pp.56-57
20 Brian Bursey. A Half Century of Progress? [A History of Economic Growth and Development in Newfoundland During the Modern Period, 1930-1980]

Faced with years of losses, the yard was given a final chance with a promise of new leadership in late 1994.[21] In late 1997, the yard was sold to the Mississippi-based Friede Goldman International for $1.

Smallwood attracted the United Kingdom giant, Albright and Wilson, to build a phosphorous reduction plant at Long Harbour [1967]. At one-third the cost of power in the United Kingdom, it was an offer the company could not refuse.[22] The rate was so attractive, concluded Brian Peckford in 1983, "that the Government could have closed the plant permanently, paid each employee $20,000 per year, and still have been money in."[23] Peckford's government renegotiated the power rate to a more "realistic" level. In the late 1980's, Albright and Wilson closed the plant.

Smallwood also provided a major push to the start of the oil refinery at Come by Chance. In the same year he announced the start of the Long Harbour project, Smallwood told the legislature the province would float a $30 million issue to begin construction of the refinery. Smallwood was intent on guaranteeing a large portion of the refinery's financing, and only backed down when a couple of his young cabinet ministers (Clyde Wells and John Crosbie) threatened to expose the deal. The refinery eventually became the biggest bankruptcy in Canadian history. Because of the action of Wells and Crosbie, the Newfoundland government avoided liability for hundreds of millions of that debt.

The establishment of these industries happened as Smallwood promoted the resettlement of people from rural areas into so-called "growth centres". He also directed substantial resources toward infrastructure development — roads, schools, Memorial University, hospitals — to make the province "conducive to economic development."[24]

The third distinct development period began under Smallwood's successor, Conservative Frank Moores, With a two-way

21 Statement from Premier Clyde Wells, Executive Council, St. John's. October 24, 1994
22 Bursey, p.421
23 Peckford, p.66
24 Bursey, p.397

emphasis on natural resources. The first was renegotiation of various resource deals completed under Smallwood, including revising the royalty structure with mining companies and a decision to buy back the shares of British Newfoundland Corporation (BRINCO). BRINCO had been given crown land and water rights concessions in 1953, including eventually, the water rights of Hamilton River Falls, later renamed Churchill Falls by Smallwood. The second part of the Moores approach to natural resources was in planning for offshore oil and gas development and for growth of fisheries infrastructure, in order to take advantage of the declaration of the 200-mile limit in 1977. The 200-mile limit gave Canada an exclusive role in managing fish resources within the new economic zone, and right of first access to major fish resources such as northern cod.

Lacking a constitutional role in the allocation and management of fish stocks, the Moores government entered an expansionist mode. A position paper titled "Fish is the Future", published in late 1978, contemplated a half billion dollars in spending by the provincial government and private sector in the six years leading up to 1984.[25] The centrepiece of the plan was to be a "superport" at Harbour Grace, where 76,000 tonnes of groundfish would be landed and "distributed to plants experiencing off-season fish shortages."[26] This plan would have addressed an old problem — putting fish in inshore plants to lengthen their processing season and expanding the number of work weeks for plantworkers. The plan was an ambitious one, aimed also at renewing old infrastructure and creating new facilities, such as vessels and plants.

Moores left political life a few months after the plan was announced. His Mines and Energy Minister, Brian Peckford, won the party leadership in March 1979 and three months later, obtained a new mandate from the electorate. In many ways, Peckford's approach to development was a continuation of the approach that emerged during the Moores years. However, Peckford's personal investment in an integrated resource development policy based on a new relationship with the federal

25 Notes for Speech delivered by the Honourable Walter Carter, Minister of Fisheries, at a Fisheries Seminar, November 13, 1978. p.6
26 Ibid, pp. 12-13

government, demands that his tenure be regarded as a fourth distinct development approach.

Peckford's approach was summed up by the words "never again", a reference to the perceived giveaway of Churchill Falls hydro and the terms under which other resources were allowed to be developed.[27] The goal was not provincial ownership of natural resources, but a channelling of effort to ensure that resources would be developed in such a way as to "raise the rates of growth in investment, employment and income to a level which will permit Newfoundland to narrow the gap that now exists between the Province and other parts of Canada."[28]

Peckford's resource development policies were centred on fisheries, hydro and offshore oil and gas development. It was an extremely high-risk strategy, since it presumed a major power shift in the Canadian state — including the eventual entrenchment of provincial management rights in fisheries in the Constitution;[29] a favourable Supreme Court decision giving ownership of offshore oil and gas to Newfoundland; and intervention from the federal government to facilitate construction of a hydro power corridor through Quebec. The government saw corrective action on all three fronts as imperative to a transformation that would strengthen the provincial economy. It stated, "the relatively undeveloped state of the goods producing sector can be attributed to the lack of manufacturing industries linked to the Province's resource base."[30]

The pursuit of these issues led to a tumultuous period in the relationship between Newfoundland and Ottawa. In the end, Newfoundland got no say over fisheries management and no power corridor through Quebec. Peckford was however, able to persuade the Mulroney Conservative government to agree to an administrative arrangement (the Atlantic Accord) on offshore oil and gas, thereby allowing the province some say over the pace of development and allowing it to choose the mode of

---

27 Government of Newfoundland and Labrador. Managing All Our Resources (A Development Plan for Newfoundland and Labrador) St. John's. October 1980. p.2
28 Ibid, p.27
29 Ibid, p.57
30 Ibid, p.11

development, a right that contributed significantly to the decision by the Hibernia consortium to construct a labour-intensive concrete production system for that oil field. Peckford regarded offshore development as "Newfoundland's last chance to become a viable society",[31] since substantial revenues from it would relieve "our debt load and heavy taxation burden so that we can have a chance to build a long term economy based on fishing and forestry."[32] In real terms though, there was a trade-off for insisting on the labour-intensive concrete production system for Hibernia. Newfoundland collects little in the way of royalties until the owners recover their pre-production costs. And even then, Newfoundland has most of those royalties deducted from the equalization payments it receives from the federal government. It will take many oil fields and a great deal more economic development related to offshore oil, to get to the point that Peckford envisioned.

Peckford left office just as major groundfish resources were entering a period of serious decline, before the Hibernia development had begun, and with no resolution to discussions on joint Labrador hydro development with Quebec (this strategy replaced a frontal attack on the Upper Churchill contract after Newfoundland's Water Rights Reversion Act was declared unconstitutional in 1984.)

Federal transfer payments, both to individuals and to the government, have been a major contributor to the province in the post-Confederation period. With the federal debt increasing substantially year over year however, Ottawa began to cut back on its expenditures in the late 1980's and into the 1990's. This approach to control federal finances impacted negatively on Newfoundland's position, with the result that provincial budgets were put under serious pressure during this period. This general situation was exacerbated by the near-total groundfish failure in the early 1990's and retrenchment in other important natural resource industries such as mining and forestry.

Peckford's departure from politics signalled the end of

31 Peckford, p.95
32 Ibid, p.104

thirty years of expansion in both the size and scope of provincial government activity in Newfoundland.

The Liberals under Clyde Wells, were returned to power in May 1989 after 17 years in opposition. They promised to help diversify the resource-dominated Newfoundland economy. This approach represented the fifth and most recent attempt to solve an old riddle — cracking the underdevelopment problem in Newfoundland.

The 1989 Liberals attempted to distance themselves from the previous interventionist approach to economic policy-making. The Liberals were philosophically inclined toward privatization of many segments of government activity (albeit, with limited success). The Wells' Liberals saw their role as setting the stage for private sector investment. This was evidenced in the production of the Strategic Economic Plan, which identified obstacles to business development in Newfoundland. The Plan was also prescriptive; one of its major immediate consequences was a package of tax incentives to attract new business to the province. A further move was the decision to consolidate a plethora of government regulatory regimes into a single "one-stop shopping" agency for permits, licenses, fees, and approvals. Government itself was reduced in size under the Wells' Liberals, although likely more as a response to budget shortfalls prompted in the main by federal cutbacks, rather than any philosophical inclination to reduce public sector employment.

The Liberals' tax incentive and tax forgiveness law — the EDGE program — was enacted in December 1994. The government paid a $2000 grant to companies for each permanent job created in industries that did not compete with firms already established in Newfoundland.[33] In implementing its policy, the

---

33 Government of Newfoundland and Labrador. Attracting New Business Investment (A White Paper on Proposed New Legislation to Promote Economic Diversification and Growth Enterprises in the Province) June 1994. p.iii [The White Paper was passed into law in December 1994. The tax incentives and tax forgiveness aspects of the White Paper remained intact. The minimum investment and sales levels required to qualify for the program were lowered after complaints that the legislation would preclude many local investors from taking part in the program. As well, a controversial section that contemplated imposing collective agreements where trade unions and employers were unable to reach agreement, was removed.]

government referred to the initiative as "bold", and stated "we must attract new investment capital and innovative industrial activity through an aggressive world-wide business prospecting and promotional initiative."[34] Wells left politics in January 1996, and in the ensuing general election, the Liberals were returned to power under Brian Tobin. The government committed itself to virtually the same economic plan as Wells, with extra emphasis on promoting Newfoundland as a good place to do business. Additionally, the Tobin government is presiding over the development of the Voisey's Bay nickel and cobalt discovery, the Hibernia offshore oil field, and the pending development of the Terra Nova and Whiterose oil fields. In the late months of 1996, the government acknowledged its earlier described "bold" tax incentive program would likely be more useful in promoting small industry rather than large businesses, since large, successful businesses would reduce the province's entitlement under the federal government's equalization program. In addition, the government discontinued the $2000 grant for each job created under the program.

In early 1998, Tobin announced an agreement-in-principle with Quebec to get more value for Newfoundland from the Upper Churchill hydro project and to develop the Gull Island part of the Lower Churchill.

CONCLUSION

Newfoundland is nearing a half-century of life inside Canada, yet the vexing problems of high unemployment and low economic growth remain. Out-migration has been a constant fact of life. Alberta and Ontario have attracted thriving communities of Newfoundlanders. Their children will no doubt have less attachment to Newfoundland than their parents. The economic problems that prompted people to leave the province preoccupies the present crop of political leaders as it did the previous officeholders.

It could be argued that Smallwood's industrialization program, while unquestionably an overall, expensive failure, did less harm to the province than his subsequent resource develop-

34 Ibid, p.iii

ment efforts with the heavy emphasis on concessions. Indeed, much of the effort in the post-Smallwood era, especially by Moores and Peckford, represented an attempt to undo some of Smallwood's resource deals. [The nationalization of BRINCO; revision of the mineral tax regime; renegotiation of the power subsidy for ERCO; and the effort to get a more favourable deal on the Upper Churchill power contract are all examples.]

The most glaring gap in the province's ability to chart its own economic course is in the area of fisheries jurisdiction. Fisheries management became a federal responsibility at Confederation, and while it is not possible to prove Newfoundland could have done better at managing the fishery, it is clear Ottawa jealously guarded its exclusive constitutional role in this area to the virtual exclusion of a meaningful advisory role for Newfoundland. Perhaps this was inevitable, given Nova Scotia's large stake in Atlantic fisheries, and its influence in regional politics. This state of affairs however, ignored economic reality in Newfoundland, where hundreds of small communities and a sizeable part of the labour force were entirely dependent on the fishery. Fish quotas were parcelled out like government grants, with little regard to the fact that hundreds of Newfoundland communities barely eked out a summer fishery from the inshore catch. Ottawa rebuffed successive attempts by Peckford, and later, by Wells, for the province to play a meaningful role in fisheries management.

By the early 1990's, the valuable groundfishery was devastated, and the hundreds of dependent Newfoundland communities faced an uncertain future. Ottawa came to their assistance with a fisheries compensation program. At the same time, it made major changes to the Unemployment Insurance program. Politicians and the mainland press often cited the fishing industry as abusers of unemployment insurance. Few were willing to trace the source of the problem — Ottawa's fisheries policy and the way it allocated quotas.

As Newfoundland nears the next millennium, promise is being held out that natural resource developments in offshore oil, Labrador hydro development, and mining will assist the province in escaping the economic and fiscal juggernaut that has gripped it so tightly. Those industries alone though, will not provide enough jobs to remove Newfoundland from the economic critical list. The province's ability to create links to service those industries will determine if the resource industries are merely job creators or if they contribute more substantially as economy builders.

An equally important indicator will be the taxes and royalties Newfoundland is able to negotiate. The province's economic past is littered with examples where developers prospered at the expense of the Newfoundland treasury. Some of the country's highest personal income and corporate taxes are in large measure a manifestation of this set of circumstances. Has the new generation of Newfoundland decision-makers learned enough from these mistakes? And are they disciplined enough to apply the brakes to attractive projects if the province does not benefit in a substantial way from resource development?

The Smallwood industrialization program stood to benefit from public scrutiny and oversight. Has Newfoundland learned these tough lessons? Will the people insist tax and royalty agreements be studied in public before final deals are signed? One does not have to go far into the past to find a litany of deals that were poorly constructed. The deal giving Quebec the option to renew its contract to buy Upper Churchill hydro power at better than 1976 rates is but one example. The Sprung greenhouse debacle is a more recent example.

Tax and royalty contributions to the treasury, and employment for Newfoundlanders, will go only part of the way toward ensuring that Newfoundland emerges from being an economically underdeveloped province. There is a troubling paradox on the way to resource wealth — the cost of providing public services for a widely dispersed population will remain high, while new resource rents will reduce the level of payments the province receives from Ottawa under the equalization program. Newfoundland is seeking an accommodation so that new resource rents are not negated by federal cuts. The outcome of this venture may determine whether pending resource development will allow the province to continue to provide a wide range of services, lower its tax rates, and possibly retire part of its debt.

Perhaps the biggest wildcard in Newfoundland's economic future is the fishery. The groundfishery, although faulted for being inefficient and perpetuating underemployment and a litany of other problems, was the single largest employer in Newfoundland until the moratorium in 1992. Admittedly, the unemployment insurance program could be credited with keeping so many people in the industry, since it effectively subsidized wages during down periods, which stretched to four-fifths of the year in some cases.

If the fishery returns, even at half the capacity and size that existed in 1992, it will contribute in a larger way than any other single industry to employment. Fisheries-related employment will contribute even more significantly to the economy if opportunities are seized to increase the value of production through further processing. If however, the cod fishery and other groundfisheries remain closed, new mines and oil development will only blunt the edge of a serious unemployment problem.

The Newfoundland development question has come full circle. The problem that vexed Smallwood in 1949, persists to this day. Out-migration remains a real, and for many, a painful phenomenon. Confederation, while beneficial for many, has not fulfilled what many hoped would be the ultimate realization — economic prosperity. Newfoundland sits at the edge of a new period of hope and promise.

And a new generation of leaders, both private and public, are about to make another try.

Will the political leaders attempt deals on Voisey's Bay and the Upper and Lower Churchill with one eye on the negotiations, and the other tuned to the timing of the next election, or some other political goal or objective? That is the crucible for politicians. The practice of politics around big projects in recent Newfoundland history does not make for contented reading.

Understanding the game of politics and economic development is a little like reading *Alice in Wonderland* — what you see is not necessarily what is there. There may not be many more occasions for Newfoundland politicians to do what is needed to set the stage to bring a level of economic prosperity.

BIBLIOGRAPHY

Alexander, David. "Development and Dependence in Newfoundland 1880-1970". Acadiensis, Vol.4, No.1. Autumn 1974

Atlantic Provinces Economic Council. Atlantic Canada Today (Halifax: Formac Publishing Limited] 1987

Baetz, Mark C. and Donald H. Thain. Canadian Cases in Business-Government Relations (Toronto: Methuen) 1985

Bassler Gerhard P. "Develop or Perish: Joseph R. Smallwood and Newfoundland's Quest for German Industry, 1949-1953". Acadiensis, Vol.15, No.2. Spring 1986

Bickerton, James. Nova Scotia, Ottawa and the Politics of Regional Development (Toronto: University of Toronto Press) 1990

Blake, Raymond B. Canadians at Last: Canada Integrates Newfoundland as a Province. (Toronto: University of Toronto Press) 1994

Brewis, T.N. Regional Economic Policies in Canada (Toronto: Macmillan) 1969

Brodie, Janine. The Political Economy of Canadian Regionalism (Toronto: Harcourt Brace Jovanovich, Canada) 1990

Browne, William J. Eight-Four Years a Newfoundlander (St. John's: Dicks and Company Limited) 1981

Bruce, Harry. Frank Sobey: The Man and the Empire (Toronto: Macmillan of Canada) 1985

Brym, Robert J. (ed.) Regionalism in Canada (Toronto: Irwin Publishing) 1986

Bursey, Brian. A Half Century of Progress? [A History of Economic Growth and Development in Newfoundland During the Modern Period, 1930-1980]

Courchene, Thomas J. "Analytical Perspectives on the Canadian economic union", in Trebilcock, M.J., and J.R.S. Prichard, T.J. Courchene, J. Whalley (eds.) Federalism and the Canadian Economic Union. (Toronto: University of Toronto Press) 1983. Published for the Ontario Economic Council. pp.51-110

George, Roy E. The Life and Times of Industrial Estates Limited (Halifax: Institute of Public Affairs, Dalhousie University) Paper No.93. 1974

Harrington, Michael F. "New and Old Industries in an Old Colony -a Review of Newfoundland's Industrial Revolution", Atlantic Advocate, September 1957. Vol.48, No.1.

Hopkins, Garth. Clairtone [The Rise and Fall of a Business Empire] (Toronto: McClelland and Stewart) 1978

Horwood, Harold. Joey (Toronto: Stoddart) 1989

Kuklinski, Anton, Olli Kultalahti and Britta Koskiaho (eds.) Regional Dynamics of Socioeconomic Change (Tempere: Finnpublishers) 1979

McAllister, R.I. Newfoundland and Labrador: The First Fifteen Years of Confederation (St. John's: Dicks and Company Limited) 1967

Martin, Michael T. and Terry R. Kandal (eds.) Studies of Development and Change in the Modern World (New York: Oxford University Press) 1989

Mathias, Philip. Forced Growth (Toronto: James Lewis and Samuel, Publishers) 1971

Mayo, H. B. Atlantic Guardian. March 1951

Neary, Peter (ed.) The Political Economy of Newfoundland, 1929-1972 (Toronto: Copp Clark Publishing) 1973

Peckford, Brian. The Past in the Present (St. John's: Harry Cuff Limited) 1983

Phidd, Richard W. and G. Bruce Doern. The Politics and Management of Canadian Economic Policy. (Toronto: Macmillan) 1978

Sager, Eric W., and Lewis R. Fischer and Stuart O. Pierson. Atlantic Canada and Confederation [Essays in Canadian Political Economy]. (Toronto: University of Toronto Press) Published in association with Memorial University of Newfoundland. 1983

Shonfield, Andrew. Modern Capitalism [The Changing Balance of Public and Private Power] (New York: Oxford University Press) 1976

Smallwood, Joseph R. I Chose Canada (Toronto: Macmillan) 1973

Journals, Newspapers

Atlantic Provinces Economic Council, Annual Reviews

Newfoundland Journal of Commerce

The *Evening Telegram*

Winnipeg Free Press

Financial Post

Maclean's Magazine

Atlantic Guardian

Atlantic Advocate

J.R. Smallwood Collection, Centre for Newfoundland Studies, Memorial University

Certified cabinet minutes

Various speeches, letters, cables, notes and memos

Minutes, Board of Directors Meetings, various industries

"Report on Superior Rubber Company" by P.P. Cow and Company Limited, November 30, 1955

Annual Financial Statements, various industries

Annual Reports, Industrial Development Loan Board

"Draft Reports and "Conclusions", various industries, Arthur D. Little Inc.

Government Documents

Newfoundland/Ottawa. Community Matters: The New Regional Economic Development. [Report of the Task Force on Community Economic Development in Newfoundland and Labrador] St. John's. January 1995. (Study funded by Atlantic Canada Opportunities Agency and Enterprise Newfoundland and Labrador)

Newfoundland. Attracting New Business Investment [A White Paper on Proposed New Legislation to Promote Economic Diversification and Growth Enterprises in the Province] St. John's. June 1994

Managing All Our Resources (St. John's) October 1980 Interim Report on Capacity to Pay and Comparative Tax Burden in Newfoundland and the Maritime Provinces". A Presentation to the Newfoundland Commission, Revision of Financial Terms, by H. Carl Goldenberg, Economic Advisor to Government of Newfoundland. January 1956

Report of the Royal Commission on the Economic State and Prospects of Newfoundland and Labrador. St. John's. 1967

Report of the Royal Commission on Employment and Unemployment. St. John's. 1985

House of Assembly Proceedings

    Throne Speeches

    Notes for a Speech, Honourable Walter Carter, Minister of Fisheries, November 13, 1978

    Statement, Premier Clyde Wells, on Future of the Marystown Shipyard, October 24, 1994

Ottawa. "The Clothing and Textiles Industries". Department of Trade and Commerce, Economics Division, Industrial Intelligence Division #2. (Undated)

Nova Scotia. "Principal Agreement Between Industrial Estates Limited and the Provincial Government". September 25, 1957

Voluntary Planning Board. First Plan for Economic Development to 1968. February 1966

Industrial Estates Limited, Annual Reports